HARCOURT HORIZONS

The Pledge of Allegiance

I pledge allegiance to the Flag

of the United States of America,

and to the Republic

for which it stands,

one Nation under God, indivisible,

with liberty and justice for all.

HARCOURT HORIZONS

About My Community

Harcourt
SCHOOL PUBLISHERS

Orlando   Austin   New York   San Diego   Toronto   London

Visit *The Learning Site!*
www.harcourtschool.com

HARCOURT HORIZONS

ABOUT MY COMMUNITY

General Editor

Dr. Michael J. Berson
Associate Professor
Social Science Education
University of South Florida
Tampa, Florida

Contributing Authors

Dr. Sherry Field
Associate Professor
The University of Texas at Austin
Austin, Texas

Dr. Tyrone Howard
Assistant Professor
UCLA Graduate School of
    Education & Information Studies
University of California at
    Los Angeles
Los Angeles, California

Dr. Bruce E. Larson
Associate Professor of Teacher
    Education and Social Studies
Western Washington University
Bellingham, Washington

Series Consultants

Dr. Robert Bednarz
Professor
Department of Geography
Texas A&M University
College Station, Texas

Dr. Robert P. Green, Jr.
Professor
School of Education
Clemson University
Clemson, South Carolina

Dr. Asa Grant Hilliard III
Fuller E. Callaway Professor
    of Urban Education
Georgia State University
Atlanta, Georgia

Dr. Thomas M. McGowan
Chairperson and Professor
Center for Curriculum
    and Instruction
University of Nebraska
Lincoln, Nebraska

Dr. John J. Patrick
Professor of Education
Indiana University
Bloomington, Indiana

Dr. Cinthia Salinas
Assistant Professor
Department of Curriculum
    and Instruction
University of Texas at Austin
Austin, Texas

Dr. Philip VanFossen
Associate Professor,
    Social Studies Education,
    and Associate Director,
    Purdue Center for
    Economic Education
Purdue University
West Lafayette, Indiana

Dr. Hallie Kay Yopp
Professor
Department of Elementary,
    Bilingual, and Reading
    Education
California State University,
    Fullerton
Fullerton, California

Classroom Reviewers

Dr. Linda Bennett
Assistant Professor
Social Studies Education
Early Childhood and Elementary
   Education Department
University of Missouri–Columbia
Columbia, Missouri

Rhonda Inzer
Teacher
Vegas Verdes Elementary School
Las Vegas, Nevada

Margaret Massengale
District Social Studies Supervisor
Cleveland Municipal School District
Cleveland, Ohio

Beverly McNair
Teacher
Hollis Hand Elementary School
La Grange, Georgia

Cathy Nelson
Elementary Social Studies
   Coordinator
Columbus City School District—
   Northgate Center
Columbus, Ohio

Nancy Pendergrass
Teacher
Jason Lee Elementary School
Portland, Oregan

Karen Ann Ricketts
Teacher
Central Elementary School
Flushing, Michigan

Linda Stephenson
Teacher
Bear Road Elementary School
North Syracuse, New York

Mable Thompson
Reading Coach
F. S. Ervin Elementary School
Pine Hill, Alabama

Sidonia Todd
Teacher
Tanglewood Elementary School
Fort Myers, Florida

Amy Walker
Teacher
Bascomb Elementary School
Woodstock, Georgia

Maps
researched and prepared by

Readers
written and designed by

Take a Field Trip
video tour segments provided by

READING RAINBOW

Acknowledgments appear in the back of this book.

Printed in the United States of America

ISBN 0-15-339616-4

1 2 3 4 5 6 7 8 9 10 032 13 12 11 10 09 08 07 06 05 04

Contents

· UNIT ·

3

Looking at the Earth

 Focus Skill Categorize

Features You Can Use

Skills

Chart and Graph Skills

Citizenship Skills

Map and Globe Skills

Reading Skills

Music and Literature

Primary Sources

Examine Primary Sources

American Documents

Biography

Geography

Heritage

Science and Technology

Charts, Graphs, and Diagrams

Maps

Atlas

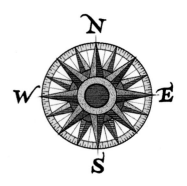

A1

ARCTIC OCEAN

Mackenzie R.

Hudson Bay

ROCKY MOUNTAINS

NORTH AMERICA

Columbia R.

Missouri R.

Great Lakes

Colorado R.

Mississippi R.

Ohio R.

APPALACHIAN MTS.

ATLANTIC OCEAN

Gulf of Mexico

PACIFIC OCEAN

Caribbean Sea

Amazon R.

SOUTH AMERICA

ANDES MOUNTAINS

PACIFIC OCEAN

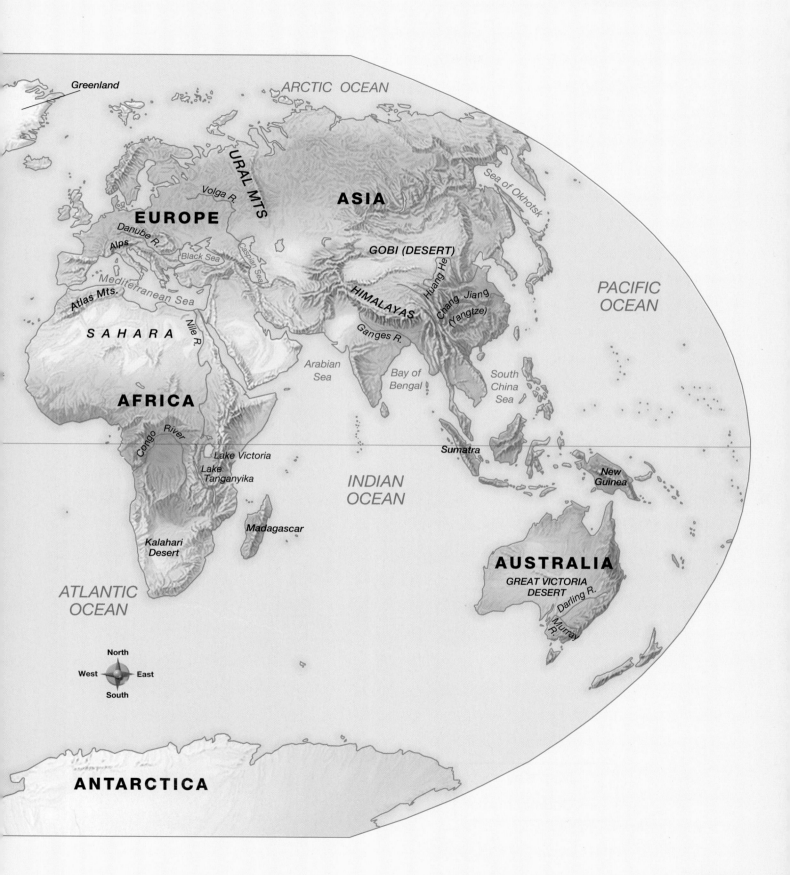

Greenland

ARCTIC OCEAN

URAL MTS.

Volga R.

EUROPE

ASIA

Danube R.

Alps

Black Sea

Caspian Sea

GOBI (DESERT)

Sea of Okhotsk

Atlas Mts.

Mediterranean Sea

HIMALAYAS

Huang He

Chang Jiang (Yangtze)

PACIFIC OCEAN

S A H A R A

Nile R.

Ganges R.

AFRICA

Arabian Sea

Bay of Bengal

South China Sea

Congo River

Lake Victoria

Sumatra

New Guinea

Lake Tanganyika

INDIAN OCEAN

Madagascar

Kalahari Desert

ATLANTIC OCEAN

AUSTRALIA

GREAT VICTORIA DESERT

Darling R.

Murray R.

North

West East

South

ANTARCTICA

A3

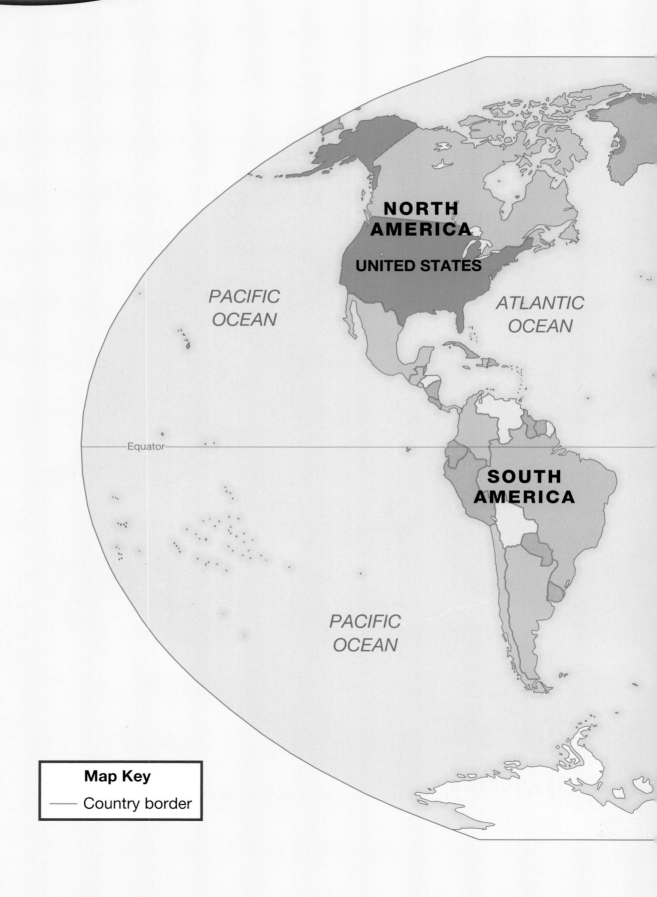

NORTH
AMERICA

UNITED STATES

PACIFIC
OCEAN

ATLANTIC
OCEAN

Equator

SOUTH
AMERICA

PACIFIC
OCEAN

Map Key

—— Country border

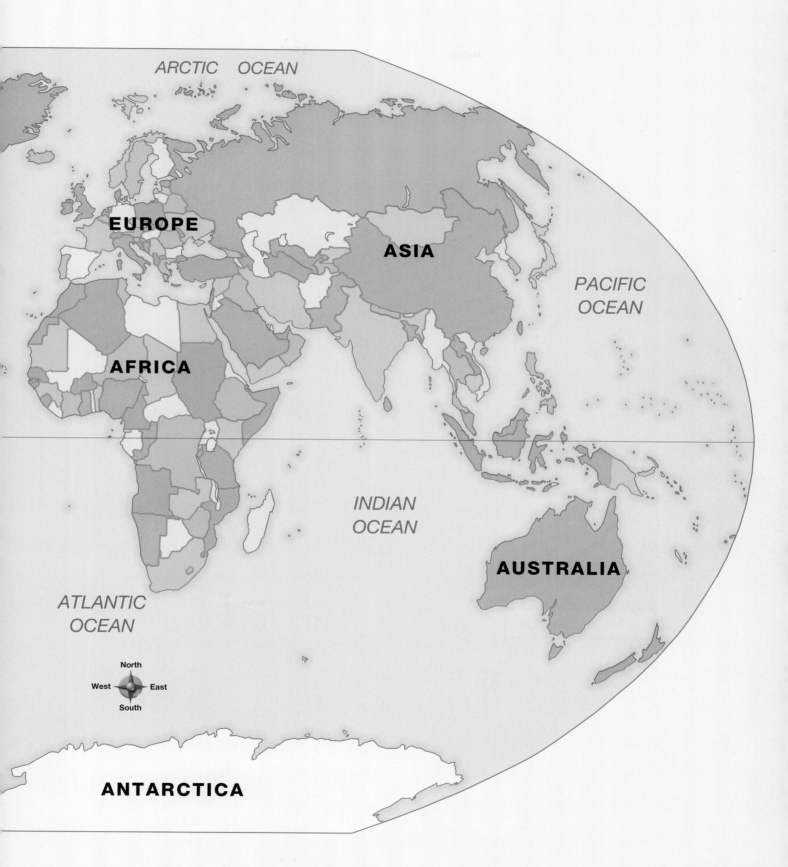

ARCTIC OCEAN

EUROPE

ASIA

PACIFIC OCEAN

AFRICA

INDIAN OCEAN

AUSTRALIA

ATLANTIC OCEAN

North
West — East
South

ANTARCTICA

A5

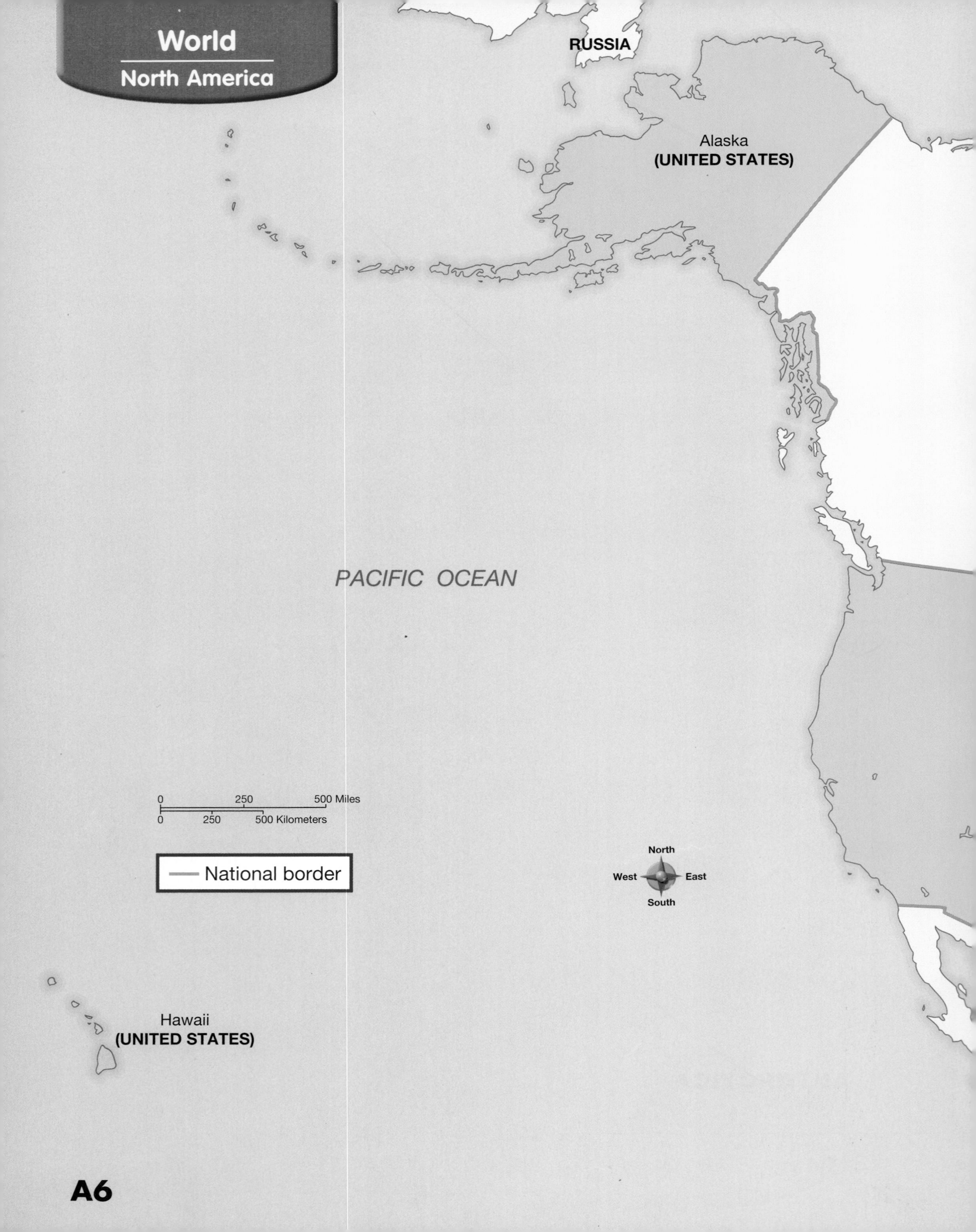

RUSSIA

Alaska
(UNITED STATES)

PACIFIC OCEAN

0   250   500 Miles
0   250   500 Kilometers

—— National border

North
West · East
South

Hawaii
(UNITED STATES)

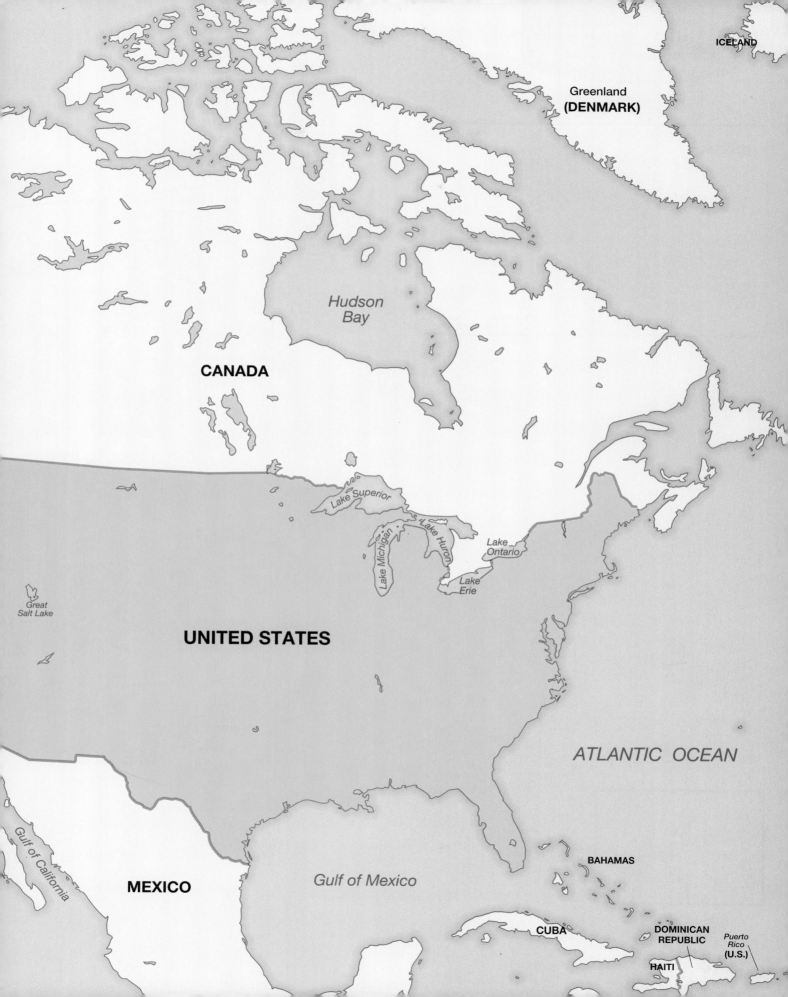

ICELAND

Greenland
(DENMARK)

Hudson
Bay

CANADA

Lake Superior

Lake Michigan

Lake Huron

Lake
Ontario

Lake
Erie

Great
Salt Lake

UNITED STATES

ATLANTIC OCEAN

Gulf of California

MEXICO

Gulf of Mexico

BAHAMAS

CUBA

DOMINICAN
REPUBLIC

Puerto
Rico
(U.S.)

HAITI

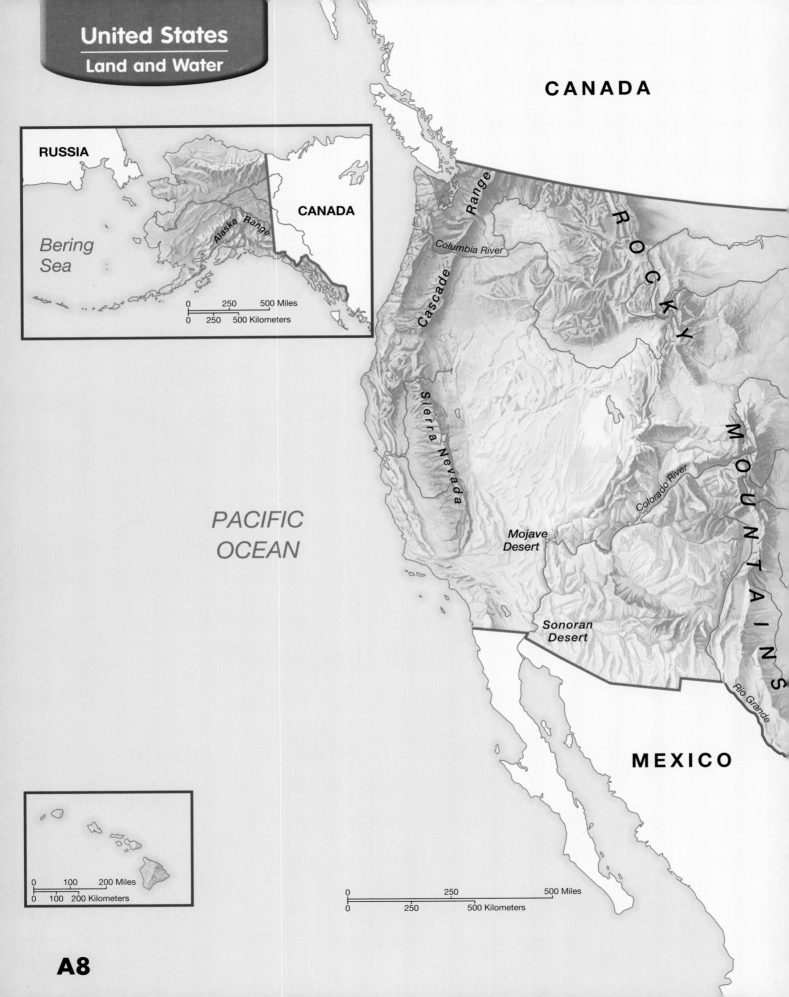

United States
Land and Water

RUSSIA

Bering Sea

CANADA

Alaska Range

| 0 | 250 | 500 Miles |
| 0 | 250 | 500 Kilometers |

CANADA

Cascade Range

Columbia River

R O C K Y

Sierra Nevada

M O U N T A I N S

*PACIFIC
OCEAN*

Colorado River

*Mojave
Desert*

*Sonoran
Desert*

Rio Grande

MEXICO

| 0 | 100 | 200 Miles |
| 0 | 100 | 200 Kilometers |

| 0 | 250 | 500 Miles |
| 0 | 250 | 500 Kilometers |

A8

CANADA

GREAT PLAINS

Missouri River

Missouri River

Mississippi River

INTERIOR
PLAINS

Missouri River

Lake Superior

Lake Michigan

Lake Huron

Lake Ontario

Lake Erie

Ohio River

APPALACHIAN MOUNTAINS

ATLANTIC
OCEAN

Mississippi River

COASTAL PLAIN

Rio Grande

North
West   East
South

Gulf of
Mexico

BAHAMAS

Straits of Florida

CUBA

A9

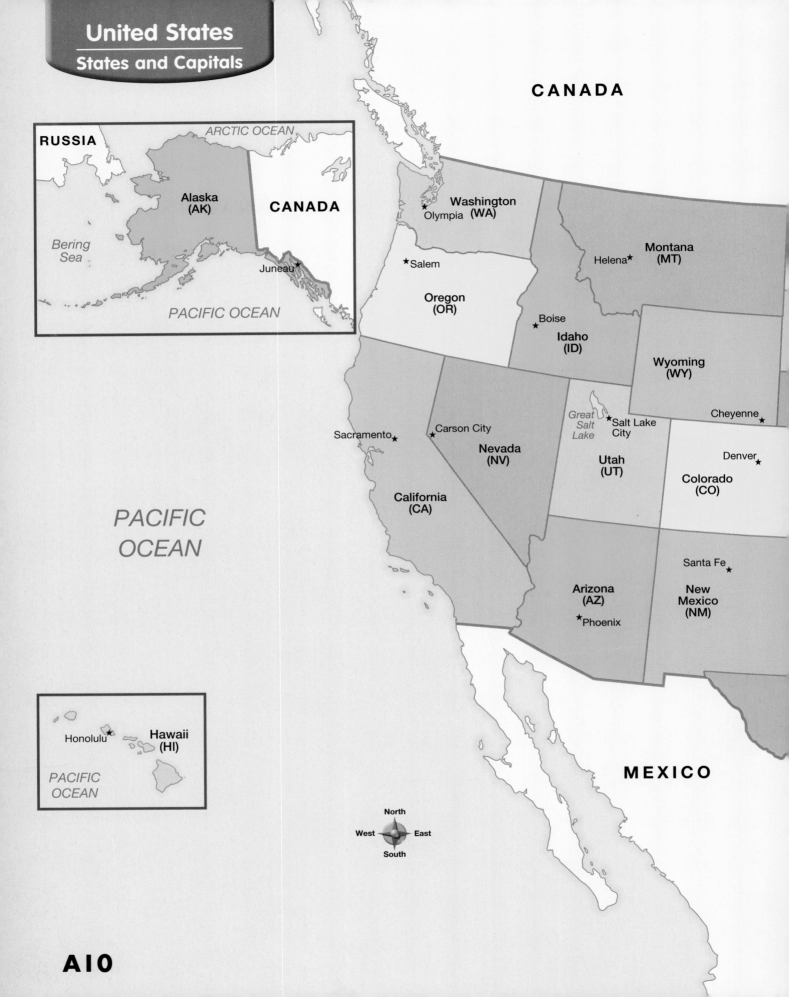

United States
States and Capitals

RUSSIA

ARCTIC OCEAN

Alaska
(AK)

CANADA

Bering
Sea

Juneau ★

PACIFIC OCEAN

CANADA

★ Olympia
Washington (WA)

★ Salem

Helena ★
Montana (MT)

Oregon
(OR)

Boise ★
Idaho
(ID)

Wyoming
(WY)

Cheyenne ★

Great
Salt
Lake
★ Salt Lake
City

Sacramento ★

★ Carson City

Nevada
(NV)

Utah
(UT)

Denver ★

Colorado
(CO)

PACIFIC
OCEAN

California
(CA)

Santa Fe ★

Arizona
(AZ)

New
Mexico
(NM)

★ Phoenix

Honolulu ★
Hawaii
(HI)

PACIFIC
OCEAN

MEXICO

North
West ⊕ East
South

A10

Geography Terms

desert a large, dry area of land

forest a large area of trees

gulf a large body of ocean water that is partly surrounded by land

hill land that rises above the land around it

island a landform with water all around it

lake a body of water with land on all sides

mountain highest kind of land

ocean a body of salt water that covers a large area

peninsula a landform that is surrounded on only three sides by water

plain flat land

river a large stream of water that flows across the land

valley low land between hills or mountains

A12

Living in a Community

A gilded eagle clock

Living in a Community

"I am a part of all that I have met."

— Alfred, Lord Tennyson, "Ulysses," 1842

 Focus Skill **Compare and Contrast**

As you read this unit, do the following.

- List the ways you live and the ways people in other communities live.
- Use the list to show how communities are alike and different.

Communities	
Alike	Different

community A group of people who live or work together in the same place. (page 6)

citizen A person who lives in and belongs to a community. (page 8)

role A part a person plays in a group or community. (page 12)

map   A drawing that shows where places are. (page 19)

cooperate   To work together. (page 16)

country   An area of land with its own people and laws. (page 22)

from
Some Things Go Together

by Charlotte Zolotow

illustrated by Brenda Joysmith

Peace with dove
Home with love

Gardens with flowers
Clocks with hours

Leaves with tree
and you with me

Mountains with high
Birds with fly

Pigeons with park
Stars with dark

Sand with sea
and you with me

Music with dance
Horses with prance

Hats with heads
Pillows with beds

Franks with beans
Kings with queens

Lions with zoo
and me with you

White with snow
Wind with blow

Moon with night
Sun with light

Sky with blue
AND ME
WITH YOU!

Think About It

1 How do friends go together?

2 Write about or draw two more things that go together.

Read a Book

Start the Unit Project

Interview a Friend   Your class will be doing interviews when you finish this unit. As you read, think about questions you would like to ask about living in your community.

Use Technology

Visit The Learning Site at **www.harcourtschool.com** for additional activities, primary sources, and other resources to use in this unit.

1

A Community of People

2. title

1. lesson number

3. text

Big Idea
People in communities need to get along with one another.

People everywhere belong to communities. A **community** is a group of people who live or work together in the same place. You belong to a school community. Your family is part of the community in which you live.

4. new word

Vocabulary

community

citizen

rule

fair

responsibility

6. caption

Atlanta, Georgia

5. picture

6

Some communities are large.
Some communities are small.
Communities are in many
different places.

Santa Fe, New Mexico

Miami, Florida

Montgomery, Alabama

FAST FACT The 1996 summer Olympics were held in Atlanta, Georgia.

A person who belongs to a community is a **citizen**. Citizens in a community follow the same rules. A **rule** says what must or must not be done.

A good rule is fair. **Fair** means done in a way that is right and honest. A good rule is one that keeps a community safe and peaceful.

SLOW

CHILDREN PLAYING

Each citizen has a responsibility to keep the community a good place in which to live. A **responsibility** is something a citizen should take care of or do.

Do NOT Litter

Take care of yourself and others.

LESSON 1 Review

Focus Skill

1 Compare and Contrast How are the communities in this lesson alike? How are they different?

2 Vocabulary What does a good **rule** do?

3 Make a list of classroom rules.

Find the Main Idea

▶ Why It Matters

When you read for information, you look for the main ideas. The **main idea** is the most important part of what you are reading.

▶ What You Need to Know

In most paragraphs the first sentence tells the main idea. Next come **details** that explain the main idea.

▶ Practice the Skill

Read the following paragraph.

1 What is the main idea of the paragraph?

2 What are two details in the paragraph?

After a big storm our town needed a new welcome sign. Travelers often drive through our town. We wanted them to stop and spend some time in our town. The town leaders held a contest to design the friendliest sign. My school entered the contest and won!

▶ Apply What You Learned

Write a paragraph. Include a main idea and at least two details.

Vocabulary

role

A Member of Different Groups

A writer named William Shakespeare said, "All the world's a stage, . . . And one man in his time plays many parts." You play many parts in your family, your school, and your community. In each group your part, or **role** , may be different.

I am a student.

Book Report
Thomas Alva Edison
1. Inventor
2. Wizard of Menlo Park
3. Electric Light

I am a brother.

I am a friend.

I am a choir member.

Children and adults have many roles. Think about your family members. What role does each person have in your home?

Chores
Make bed ☐
Feed cat ☐
Set table ☑
Empty trash ☐
Fold clothes ☐

I am an active member of my community.

Community Roles

❶ **Vocabulary** What are some of your **roles**?

❷ How will your roles be different when you are older?

❸ Act out a role you play in the community.

Work Together

Vocabulary

cooperate

▶ Why It Matters

For some jobs in school you work alone. For other jobs you work in a group. To get the job done, each group member must **cooperate**, or work together, with others.

▶ What You Need to Know

Group members can follow these steps to help them cooperate.

Step 1 Plan together.

Step 2 Act together.

Step 3 Talk together about your work.

▶ Practice the Skill

Suppose your teacher asks your group to make a bulletin board about school and community rules. Work in your group to list some things you might do under each step.

Rules to Follow

Respect Others
Raise your hand.
Line up.
Ask before taking.
Walk on sidewalk, not grass.
Do not interrupt.

Be Safe
Look before crossing.
Stop on red; go on green.
Wear helmets and pads.
Walk, don't run.
Do not play in traffic.

▶ Apply What You Learned

With your group members, follow the steps for working together to make a new classroom rule.

3

Around the Neighborhood

Big Idea
People share places in the neighborhood.

Vocabulary

neighborhood

map

location

Think about your **neighborhood**, the part of your community in which you live. Does your neighborhood have a school, a grocery store, a library, a fire station, a park, and a bank? These are places that people share in a neighborhood. You can learn about a neighborhood by looking at a picture.

You can also learn about a neighborhood by looking at a map. A **map** is a drawing. It shows **location**, or where places are. There are many kinds of maps. A map can help you find your way from one place to another.

GEOGRAPHY THEME

How do photographs taken from above help map makers?

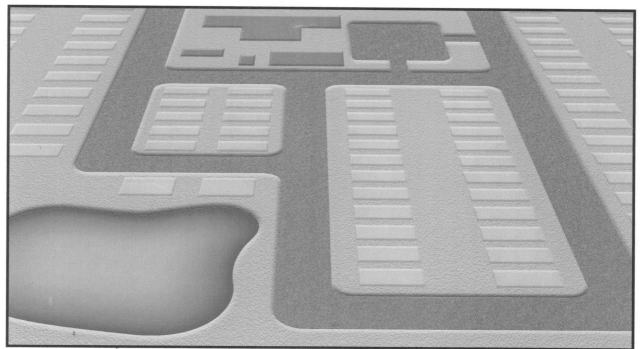

LESSON 3
Review

1 **Vocabulary** What would you see on a walk through your **neighborhood**?

2 How is a map different from a photograph?

3 Make a map of your school or neighborhood.

A Citizen of Many Communities

Big Idea
You are a citizen of your city, state, and country.

Vocabulary
city
suburb
state
country

Patty is making a model of the homes, buildings, and streets in her neighborhood. Patty's neighborhood is part of the city of Pittsburgh. A **city** is a very large town.

Pittsburgh
Understanding Places and Regions

Pittsburgh is located where the Ohio, Allegheny, and Monongahela rivers join. Bridges connect downtown Pittsburgh to its many suburbs. A **suburb** is a community near a large city.

Locate It
United States

Pittsburgh,
Pennsylvania

Together many cities, towns, and smaller communities form a **state** . Patty lives in the state of Pennsylvania. Our country has 50 states, or parts. The United States of America is our country. A **country** is an area of land with its own people and its own rules.

Patty is a citizen of the city of Pittsburgh and of the state of Pennsylvania. She is also a citizen of the United States of America.

Lawrenceville (neighborhood)

STOP

Mintwood Street

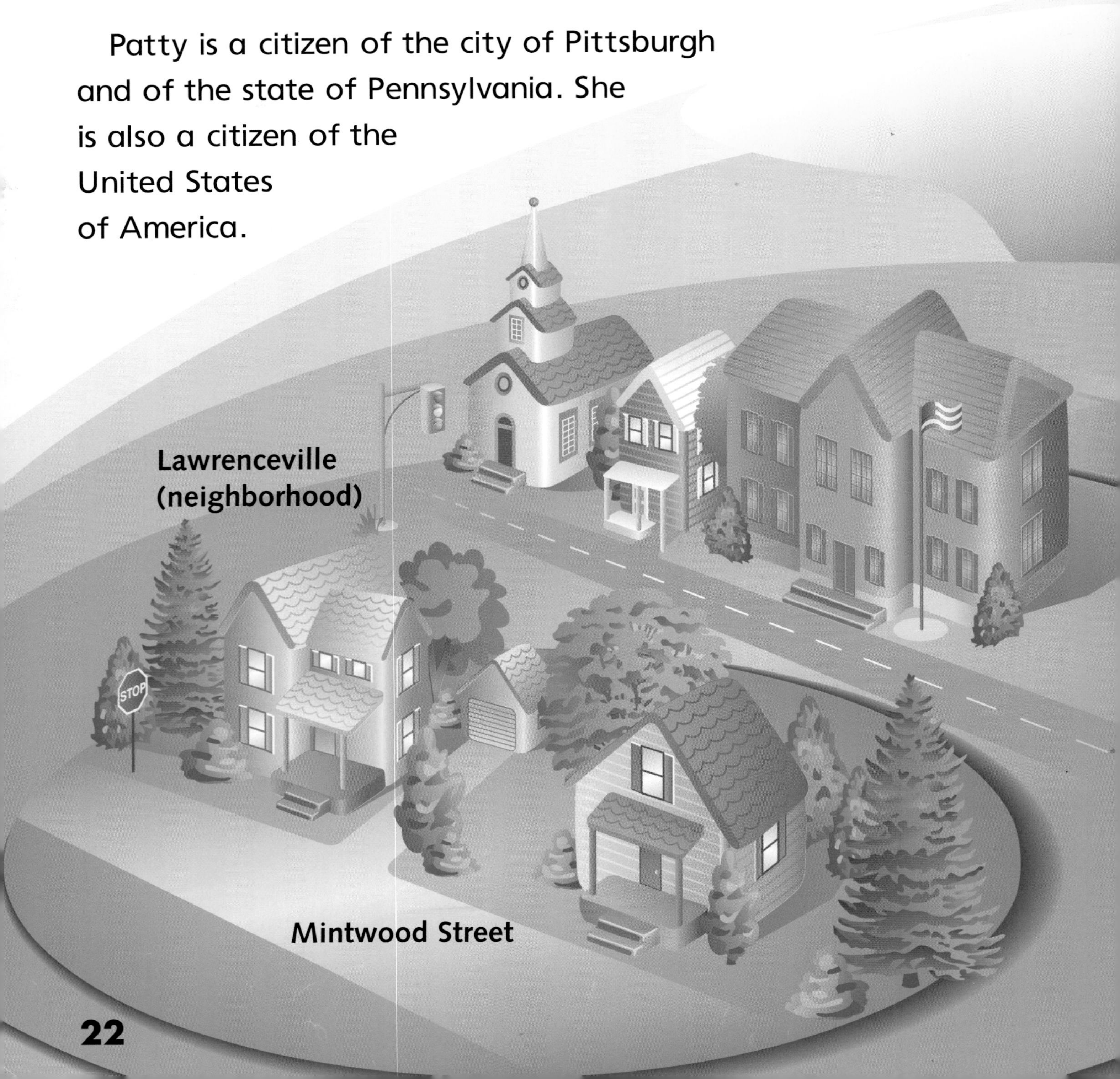

Which is larger, our country or our state?

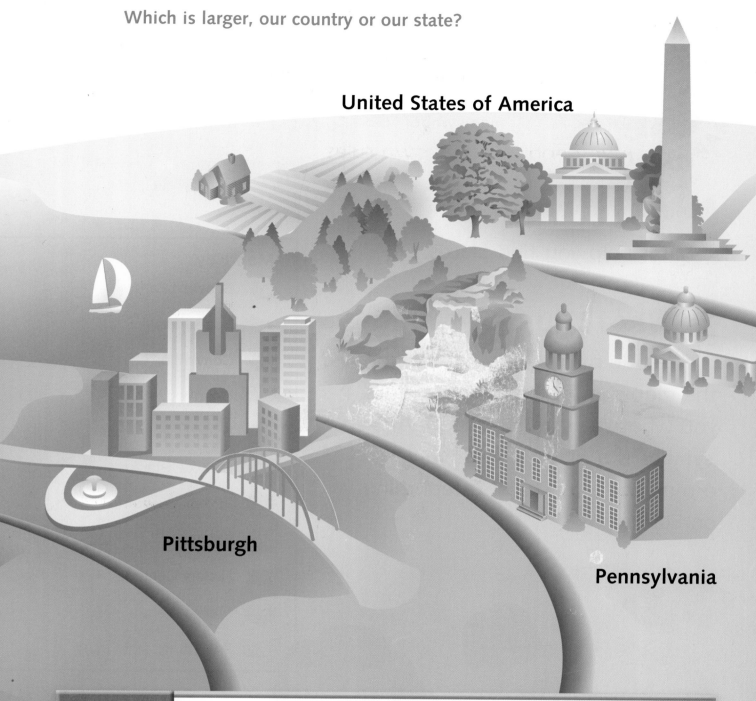

United States of America

Pittsburgh

Pennsylvania

1 **Vocabulary** In what **state** do you live?

2 How is a city different from a town?

3 Locate your community, state, and country on a map.

Read a Map Key

▶ ## Why It Matters

Maps help you find places.

▶ ## What You Need to Know

The title of a map tells you what the map shows. The **map key** tells you what the symbols mean. A **map symbol** is a picture or drawing on a map that stands for a real thing on Earth.

Map Key

 Baseball Park

 Bus Terminal

 Convention Center

 Courthouse

 Duquesne University

 Football Stadium

 Ft. Pitt Museum

 Fountain

 History Center

 Mellon Arena

PAT PAT Transit (light rail)

24

Practice the Skill

1. What is the title of this map?

2. What symbols are shown in the map key?

3. On what street is the History Center?

4. What street would you take to get from the Courthouse to Market Square?

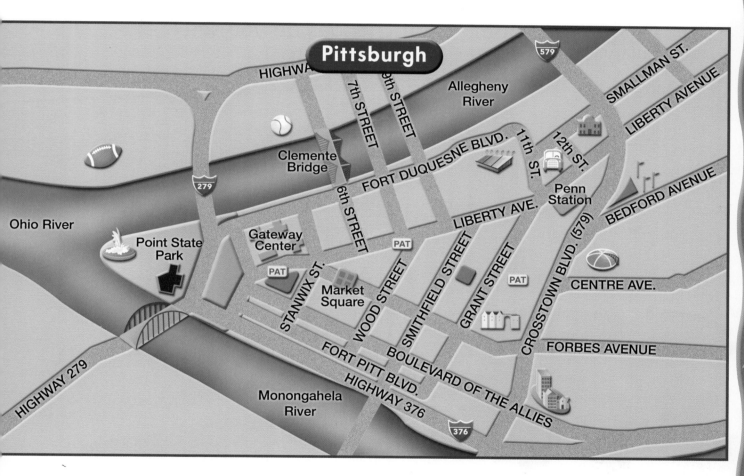

Apply What You Learned

Make a map of your city or town. Add a title and a map key.

Practice your map and globe skills with the **GeoSkills CD-ROM**.

About Change

People **change** , or become different, over time. We grow older. We grow bigger. Families also change. Look at this family album. What changes do you see?

Alice Austen   1866–1952
Character Trait: Individualism

At age 10 Alice Austen learned to use a wooden box to take pictures. From then on she was a photographer. She became one of the first women to take real-life pictures. For many years she showed the changes in our country through her photographs.

MULTIMEDIA BIOGRAPHIES
Visit The Learning Site at **www.harcourtschool.com** to learn about other famous people.

GO ONLINE

HOUSE FOR SALE BY OWNER

27

Ships brought people and supplies to South Carolina.

Places also change over time. Looking at pictures from different times can help you see how a place has changed. You can also see what has stayed the same. What do you see that is different in these pictures? What is the same in both pictures?

Charleston, South Carolina, today

CITY MARKET
HERE WAS ERECTED BETWEEN 1788 AND 1804, A PUBLIC MARKET ON LAND CEDED TO CITY COUNCIL BY CHARLES COTESWORTH PINCKNEY ET AL. WORK OF FILLING IN LOW GROUND AND CREEK COMPLETED IN 1807: AND SIX BLOCKS OF BUILDINGS CONSTRUCTED EXTENDING FROM MEETING STREET TO THE COOPER RIVER: IN ORDER, THE BEEF MARKET, THREE BUILDINGS FOR VEGETABLES, FRUIT AND OTHER PROVISIONS, A MARKET FOR SMALL MEATS, AND THE FISH MARKET.
MARKET HALL ERECTED 1841, NOW HOUSES THE CONFEDERATE MUSEUM.
PLACED BY THE CITY OF CHARLESTON
NOVEMBER 20, 1939

Signs like this one can be found in historic places in a community.

LESSON 5
Review

 Focus Skill

① Compare and Contrast How have you changed since last year? How have you stayed the same?

② Vocabulary How does a place **change**?

③ Write a news story about a change in a family, school, or neighborhood.

Use a Calendar

Vocabulary

calendar

▶ Why It Matters

A **calendar** is a chart that shows days, weeks, and months in a year. A calendar measures time.

▶ What You Need to Know

Each calendar page has a title. The title tells you what month it is. Rows go across a calendar page. They show the number of weeks in a month. Columns go down the page. They show the days of the week. Each day in a month is numbered. You read a date on a calendar as month, day, year—for example, August 6, 2005.

September

Sunday Sun.	Monday Mon.	Tuesday Tues.	Wednesday Wed.	Thursday Thurs.	Friday Fri.	Saturday Sat.
			1		2 Christa McAuliffe	3
4 Lewis Howard Latimer	5 Labor Day	6 School begins	7 Grandma Moses	8 la la la	9	10
11	12 Open House	13	14	15	16	17
18	19 Guest Speaker	20	21	22 la la la	23	24
25	26 John Chapman	27	28	29	30	

▶ Practice the Skill

1 What month is shown?

2 How many days are in this month?

3 On what day is the guest speaker coming?

4 What day of the week is September 1?

5 What is going to happen on September 12?

▶ Apply What You Learned

Make calendar pages for the next two months. Show some things you will do at school and any important days.

Needs and Wants

Big Idea
Everyone has needs and wants.

Vocabulary

need

want

People work together to meet their needs. A **need** is something they must have to live. All people need food, clothing, and a safe place to live.

Needs

Besides needs, people have wants. A **want** is something they would like to have but do not need. Toys and games are wants. What are some others?

People cannot have everything they want. They have to decide what things they want most and what they can do without.

Wants

LESSON 6
Review

❶ **Vocabulary** What is the difference between a **want** and a **need**?

❷ What are three things everyone needs?

❸ Write in your journal something you want. Tell what you would do without to get it.

VISIT A Community *Mural*

Get Ready

Community projects bring together people who want to help their neighborhood. People may create a mural, or large wall painting, for their community to enjoy. In California more than four hundred people worked together to paint this mural, *The Great Wall of Los Angeles*. It shows the history of communities in California.

Locate It
United States

California

What to See

Artists sketch parts of the mural on the wall. Many people must work together to create a mural.

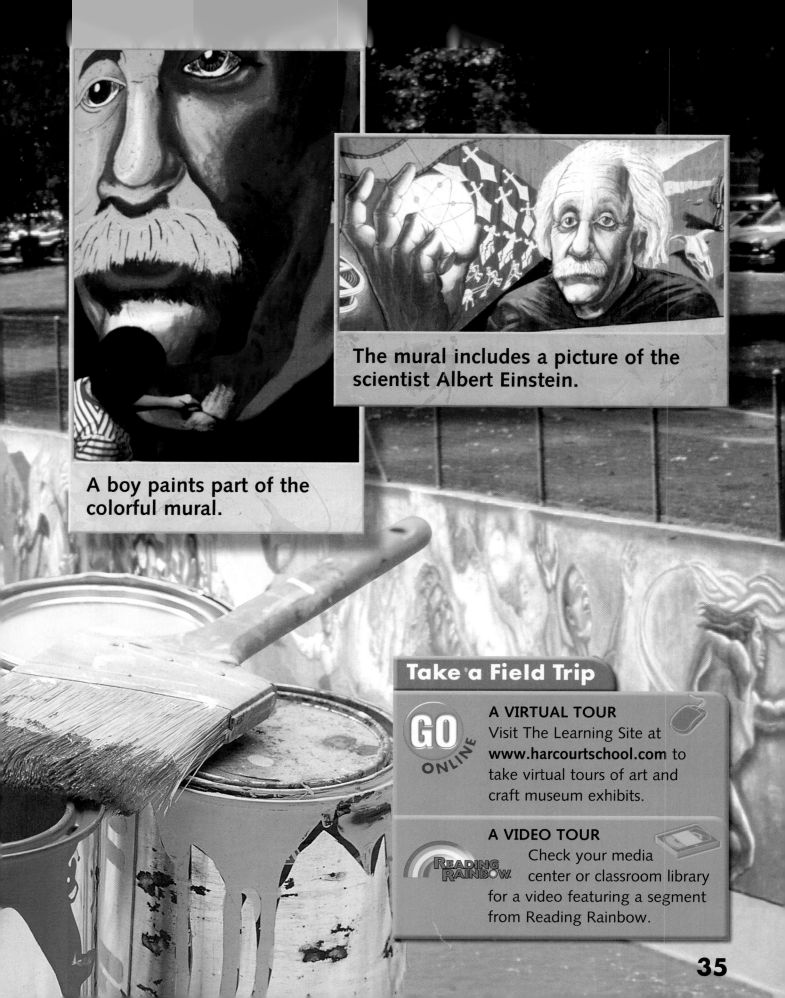

The mural includes a picture of the scientist Albert Einstein.

A boy paints part of the colorful mural.

Take a Field Trip

GO ONLINE

A VIRTUAL TOUR
Visit The Learning Site at **www.harcourtschool.com** to take virtual tours of art and craft museum exhibits.

READING RAINBOW

A VIDEO TOUR
Check your media center or classroom library for a video featuring a segment from Reading Rainbow.

Focus Skill **Compare and Contrast**

Use what you have learned to fill in the chart about communities. Think about things such as people's roles, changes, and needs and wants.

Communities

Alike	Different
1. People live in communities.	1. Some communities are small.
2. Everyone belongs to groups.	2. Adults' roles are different from children's roles.
3.	3.
4.	

THINK & WRITE

Choose a Group Think about a group to which you belong. What does the group do? What is your role in the group?

Write a Main Idea Write a sentence that tells the main idea about your group. Add two or three details that explain the main idea.

Use Vocabulary

Write the correct words to complete the paragraph.

Our **❶** _____ is the United States of America. Everyone has a **❷** _____ to play in the **❸** _____ in which he or she lives. A good **❹** _____ must work together, or **❺** _____, with others.

citizen
(p. 8)
community
(p. 6)
cooperate
(p. 16)
country
(p. 22)
role
(p. 12)

Recall Facts

❻ Why are rules important?

❼ Name two places in a neighborhood that people share.

❽ How do families change?

❾ A small community near a big city is called a—

  A country.   **B** suburb.

  C neighborhood.   **D** map.

❿ People's basic needs are—

  F games, books, and movies.

  G work, play, and sleep.

  H food, shelter, and clothing.

  J family, school, and community.

11 What responsibilities do you have in school?

12 Why are people's wants different?

Apply Chart and Graph Skills

November

Sunday	Monday	Tuesday	Wednesday	Thursday	Friday	Saturday
		1	2 Día de los Muertos	3	4	5 Guy Fawkes Day
6 John Philip Sousa's Birthday	7	8	9	10	11 Veterans Day	12
13	14 Robert Fulton's Birthday	15	16	17	18	19
20	21	22	23	24 Thanksgiving	25	26
27	28	29	30			

13 What month of the year is shown on the calendar?

14 How many days are in this month?

15 On what date is Robert Fulton's birthday?

16 What holiday is celebrated on November 11?

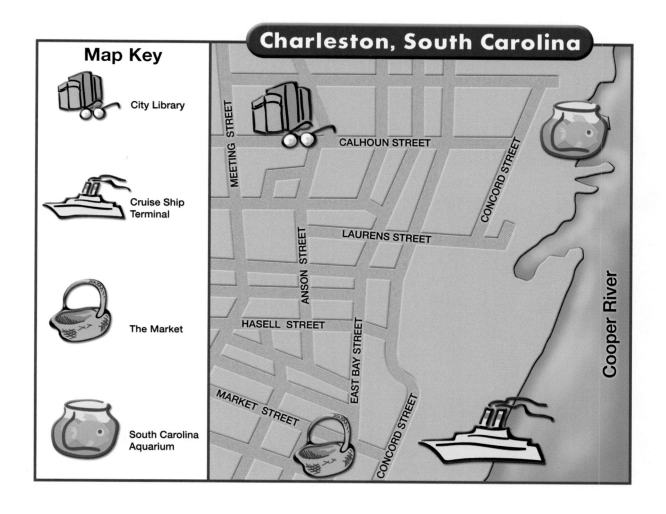

Map Key

City Library

Cruise Ship Terminal

The Market

South Carolina Aquarium

Charleston, South Carolina

MEETING STREET

CALHOUN STREET

CONCORD STREET

ANSON STREET

LAURENS STREET

HASELL STREET

EAST BAY STREET

MARKET STREET

CONCORD STREET

Cooper River

17 What does this map show?

18 What symbol stands for the South Carolina Aquarium?

19 On what street is the City Library?

20 What would you find on Market Street?

Unit Activities

GO ONLINE

Visit The Learning Site at
www.harcourtschool.com
for additional activities.

Complete the Unit Project Work with a partner to finish the unit project. Take turns interviewing classmates or friends and neighbors about living in your community.

Plan Your Interview

Make a list of questions, such as:
- What do you like about our community?
- What has changed in our community?
- To what groups do you belong?

Report Your Findings

Share the answers to your interview questions with classmates. Compare your answers. Discuss how the answers are alike and different.

Visit Your Library

Teamwork by Ann Morris. People all over the world cooperate to meet a goal or complete a project.

Mei-Mei Loves the Morning by Margaret Holloway Tsubakiyama. People everywhere share the same needs.

Bravo, Maurice! by Rebecca Bond. As Maurice watches his family at work, he discovers his own special talent.

40

Our Government

Uncle Sam's Hat
coin bank

2

Our Government

❝ The government is us: we are the government; you and I. **❞**

— Theodore Roosevelt, in a speech, 1902

(Focus Skill) Prior Knowledge

Before you read this unit, do the following.
- List what you already know about government and citizenship.
- List what you want to know about government and citizenship.

As you read this unit, do the following.
- List what you learned about government and citizenship.

K-W-L Chart

What I Know	What I Want to Know	What I Learned

government A group of citizens that runs a community, state, or country. (page 47)

Molly's Pet Store

Order Number 14432

At Molly's, Service Is Number One

Fish Tank	22.49
Goldfish	1.49
Gravel	2.49
Fish Food	1.99
4 Items Subtotal	28.46
Sales Tax 6%	1.71
Total	30.17
Cash Payment	31.00
Change	.83

Save all receipts
THANK YOU

law A rule that people in a community must follow. (page 48)

tax Money paid to the government that is used to pay for services. (page 56)

patriotism   A feeling of pride people have for their country. (page 74)

vote   A choice that gets counted. (page 60)

America the Beautiful

by Katharine Lee Bates
illustrated by Ande Cook

O beautiful for spacious skies,
For amber waves of grain,
For purple mountain majesties
Above the fruited plain!

America! America!
God shed His grace on thee
And crown thy good with brotherhood
From sea to shining sea!

Think About It

1. What did Katharine Lee Bates think was beautiful about America?

2. Draw a picture that shows something you think is beautiful about your country.

Read a Book

Start the Unit Project

Citizenship Role Plays You will meet many people as you read this unit. Think about their roles as good citizens of our country. At the end of the unit, you will work with others to role-play their actions for the class.

Use Technology

GO ONLINE Visit The Learning Site at **www.harcourtschool.com** for additional activities, primary sources, and other resources to use in this unit.

1

Big Idea
People follow laws made by their governments.

Vocabulary

government

law

consequence

Getting Along in a Community

In "America the Beautiful," we sing, "and crown thy good with brotherhood." Brotherhood means getting along with each other. Citizens need to get along to keep their communities safe and peaceful.

To keep order and to keep people safe, each community has a government. A **government** is a group of citizens that runs a community.

A government makes laws. It also makes sure the laws are obeyed. A **law** is a rule that people in a community must follow. Laws tell citizens what to do and what not to do. Traffic laws, for example, tell people where to walk and where not to walk. Without laws, people might be hurt. They might cross a street and be hit by cars.

PED
XING

All the people in a community must obey the same laws. If they break the laws, they will face consequences. A **consequence** is something that happens because of what a person does. Being hurt in an accident is one kind of consequence. Having to pay a fine, or money, is another kind of consequence. If a person breaks a very important law, he or she may have to go to jail.

This community has a leash law for dogs.

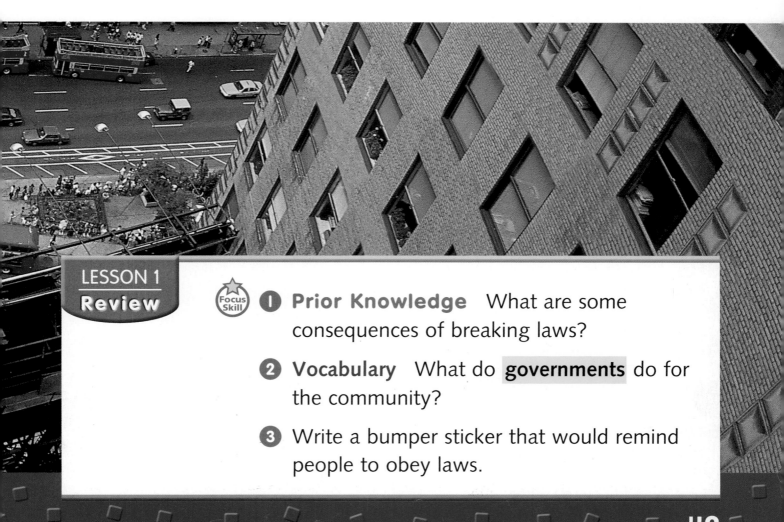

LESSON 1 Review

(Focus Skill)

❶ **Prior Knowledge** What are some consequences of breaking laws?

❷ **Vocabulary** What do **governments** do for the community?

❸ Write a bumper sticker that would remind people to obey laws.

Skills

CITIZENSHIP

Solve Problems

Vocabulary

problem

solution

▶ Why It Matters

Citizens in a community work together to find answers to problems. A **problem** is something difficult or hard to understand.

▶ What You Need to Know

A **solution** is the way people agree to find answers to, or solve, a problem.

There are steps you can follow to solve a problem.

Step 1   Name the problem.

Step 2   Gather information.

Step 3   Think about different solutions.

Step 4   Think about consequences.

Step 5   Try a solution.

Step 6   Think about how well you solved the problem.

▶ Practice the Skill

Look at the picture. Name the problem that you think needs to be solved. Think of some solutions.

▶ Apply What You Learned

Choose a way to show your ideas to the class. You might make a model, write a story, or draw a picture.

Community Governments

Most community governments are made up of three parts. Some communities have a mayor. A **mayor** is a leader of a city or town government. The mayor makes sure things get done that will make the community a good place to live.

Connie Marshall is the mayor of Bellevue, Washington

Bellevue City Council

In some communities, a group of citizens is chosen to make choices for all the people. This group is called a city or town **council**. A council meets to talk about and solve problems. In many communities, the council and a mayor make laws.

Town Meetings

In some small towns, all the people help to govern. They meet in a school, church, or town hall. Everyone gets a chance to talk. The townspeople might discuss buying a new garbage truck or land for a new park.

Courts are another part of community government. A **court** decides whether a person has broken a law and, if so, what the consequence should be. A **judge** is a person in charge of a court. Judges make sure that citizens are treated fairly.

You know that in an emergency you should call 911. Fire and police departments will come to help. They are government services. A **government service** is something that the government provides for all the citizens of a community. Other government services include schools, libraries, and parks.

Community governments can provide services because the community's citizens pay taxes. A **tax** is money paid to the government to pay for services. The government uses tax money to fix streets and to buy police cars and fire engines.

How do these services make your community a good place to live?

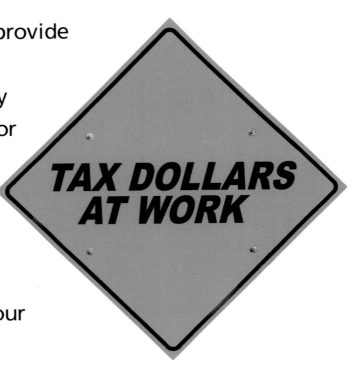

TAX DOLLARS AT WORK

1. **Vocabulary** What are some **government services**?

2. What is the mayor's job?

3. Write three questions you might use to interview your mayor, a city council member, or a judge.

Choosing Leaders

Big Idea
Americans choose their leaders.

Vocabulary
election
vote
appointed

Leaders have always been important to communities. They built cities and made laws. Long ago, however, leaders were not chosen by the people. Some leaders were born to lead. They grew up to take the place of their parents who were leaders before them. Others became leaders by winning wars.

Leaders Long Ago

In a part of Africa named Egypt, leaders were called pharaohs. Ramses II was a pharaoh. His family led Egypt for hundreds of years. Ramses II ruled for 67 years.

Ramses II made thousands of workers build huge statues and buildings. Some of these can still be seen today.

Kublai Khan led a huge army to control a large part of Asia called China. As leader he planned roads and waterways so people could travel to get things they needed. Later, a European trader named Marco Polo went to China. He brought back amazing stories about the cities the Chinese people had built.

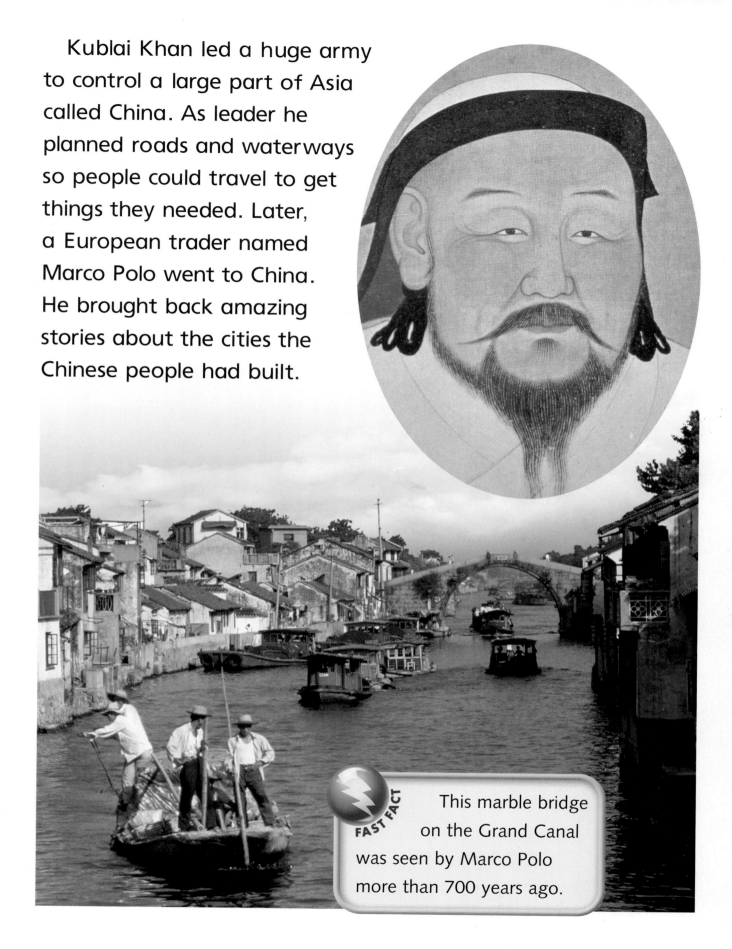

FAST FACT This marble bridge on the Grand Canal was seen by Marco Polo more than 700 years ago.

Leaders Today

In our country, we have no pharaohs who are born to lead. Our leaders are not generals who won wars against us. Citizens of the United States choose their leaders in an election. An **election** is a time when people vote for their leaders. A **vote** is a choice that gets counted.

In an election, the person who gets the most votes wins. Voting is a fair way for groups to make choices.

The people elected to be our leaders can choose people to help them. These people are **appointed**, or given their jobs by the leaders. Citizens do not vote for them.

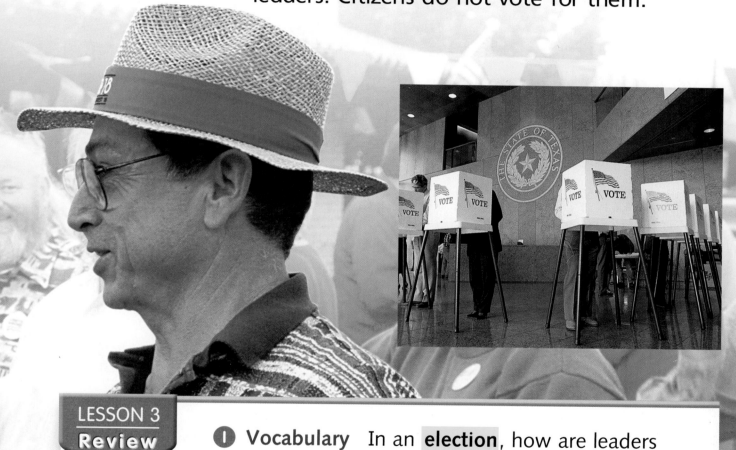

LESSON 3
Review

❶ **Vocabulary** In an **election**, how are leaders selected?

❷ How is the way people become leaders in our country today different from the ways people became leaders long ago?

❸ Make a list of reasons you might choose someone for a leader.

Make a Choice by Voting

Vocabulary

majority rule

ballot

▶ Why It Matters

Voting is a way a group of people can choose what most of them want. This is called **majority rule**. Majority means "more than half."

▶ What You Need to Know

1 Before people vote, they think about who will do the best job.

2 To vote in most elections, people mark a ballot. A **ballot** is a piece of paper used in voting. It lists all the choices, and voters mark just one. Ballots are kept secret until everyone has voted.

3 After the voting is finished, the votes are counted. The winner is the one that gets the most votes.

▶ Practice the Skill

BEFORE Imagine that your classroom is a community that needs a new mayor. Four people want to be the community's leader, but only one can be the mayor.

DURING Make ballots with the names on them. Pass them out to the class.

AFTER Once everyone has marked his or her ballots, count the votes. The person who gets the most votes wins.

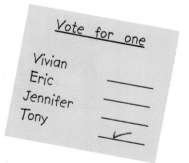

Vivian	Eric	Jennifer	Tony
卌 |||	卌 卌 卌	|||	卌

Vote for one

Vivian
Eric ____
Jennifer ____
Tony ____ ✓

▶ Apply What You Learned

Use voting as a way of making other choices in your classroom.

Our State Governments

Big Idea
Every state has its own government.

Like a community, a state has citizens who make laws, carry them out, and see that they work fairly. Each state government has a leader called a governor. The **governor** of a state is like a mayor of a city or town. The governor suggests laws and sees that all state laws are obeyed.

Ella Grasso

Ella Grasso of Connecticut was the first woman elected governor.

Franklin Roosevelt

Seventeen governors became President of the United States. Franklin Roosevelt of New York was one of them.

The state **legislature** is like a city council but much larger. This group of elected citizens makes laws for the state. Members of the legislature come from the cities and towns around the state. They work to make laws that are fair for everybody. People from other states must obey the laws of the state they are in.

The state also has courts. Judges in state courts decide when state laws have been broken. Some judges are elected. Others are appointed.

City and state governments do different jobs. State governments, for example, decide how many days children will go to school. They build highways and take care of the land and water in the state. State government services help some people meet their needs for food and shelter.

City and state governments each have police who protect citizens and their property. **Property** is what belongs to a person or a group. Often when there is a bad storm or flood, the state helps people whose property is damaged.

A state's National Guard is called to help in emergencies.

LESSON 4
Review

Focus Skill

① **Prior Knowledge** Why do cities and states need laws?

② **Vocabulary** Who is the **governor** of your state?

③ Write a letter to your state lawmakers. Ask them questions about their jobs.

Skills — MAP AND GLOBE

Find States and Capitals

Vocabulary
border
capital

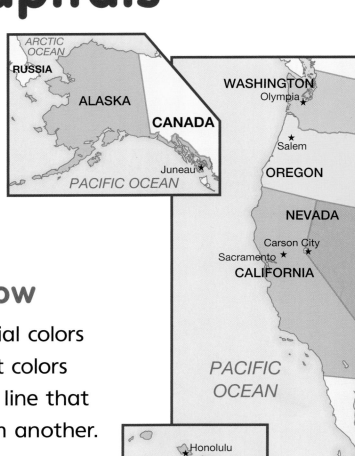

▶ Why It Matters

You can find cities and states on a map.

▶ What You Need to Know

On many maps, states have special colors to tell one from the other. Different colors help you see borders. A **border** is a line that separates one state or country from another.

Capitals have a special symbol. It is usually a star. A **capital** is a city where the government of a state or country is located.

▶ Practice the Skill

1 Find your state. What is its capital city?

2 Of what state is Boston the capital?

3 Name the states that share a border with Tennessee.

United States

NEW HAMPSHIRE
CANADA
VERMONT
MAINE
★ Augusta
Helena
★
MONTANA
NORTH DAKOTA
★ Bismarck
MINNESOTA
Lake Superior
Montpelier ★
Concord
★ Boston
NEW YORK
SOUTH DAKOTA
St. Paul
Lake Huron
Lake Ontario
Albany ★
MASSACHUSETTS
Boise ★
IDAHO
★ Pierre
WISCONSIN
Madison ★
MICHIGAN
Lansing ★
Lake Erie
Hartford ★
RHODE ISLAND
Providence
WYOMING
IOWA
Des Moines
PENNSYLVANIA
Harrisburg ★
CONNECTICUT
Trenton
Cheyenne
★
NEBRASKA
Lincoln ★
INDIANA
OHIO
Columbus
NEW JERSEY
Dover
Salt Lake City
Denver ★
Lake Michigan
ILLINOIS
Springfield
Indianapolis
Annapolis
DELAWARE
UTAH
COLORADO
Topeka ★
Jefferson City ★
WEST VIRGINIA
★ Charleston
Washington, D.C.
MARYLAND
KANSAS
MISSOURI
Richmond
ARIZONA
Frankfort
KENTUCKY
VIRGINIA
Santa Fe ★
OKLAHOMA
★
ARKANSAS
Nashville
TENNESSEE
Raleigh ★
NORTH CAROLINA
NEW MEXICO
Oklahoma City
Little ★
Rock
ALABAMA ★ Atlanta
Columbia
SOUTH CAROLINA
Phoenix ★
MISSISSIPPI
GEORGIA
ATLANTIC OCEAN
TEXAS
LOUISIANA
Jackson
Montgomery
★
★ Tallahassee
Austin ★
Baton Rouge ★
FLORIDA
MEXICO
North
West ✦ East
South
Gulf of Mexico

Map Key
⊛ National capital
★ State capital
— Border

▶ **Apply What You Learned**

List the capitals of all the states that share a border with your state.

Practice your map and globe skills with the **GeoSkills CD-ROM**.

Our Country's Government

Big Idea
Our country's government has worked well for more than two hundred years.

Vocabulary

Congress

President

Supreme Court

Constitution

rights

Our country's government has three parts, or branches, just like the community and state governments you read about. Each branch has its own job to do. One branch makes the laws. Another branch carries out the laws. The third branch sees that the laws are obeyed and that they work fairly. The people who govern our country work in Washington, D.C., the capital of the United States.

Who makes our country's laws?

Government			
	Community	State	Country
Makes laws	city council	state legislature	Congress
Carries out laws	mayor	governor	President
Sees that laws work fairly	city court	state court	Supreme Court

Congress is one branch of our country's government. Congress is a group of elected lawmakers. These lawmakers come from communities all over the country. They make the laws we need to keep order and keep people safe.

Congress meets in the Capitol.

The **President** is the elected leader of the branch of government that carries out laws. The President's job is to see that things get done to make the country a good place to live. Do you know the name of our President?

The President lives in the White House.

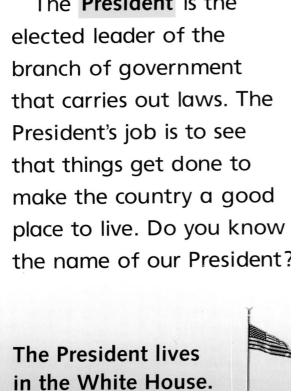

After laws are made and carried out, the courts decide if the laws are working fairly. The **Supreme Court** is the highest court in the United States. It is made up of nine appointed judges.

The **Constitution** is a written set of rules that our government must follow. This important paper explains how our government works. It also lists the **rights**, or freedoms, citizens have. Some of these rights are freedom of speech, freedom of religion, freedom of the press, and the right to meet peacefully.

LESSON 5 Review

1. **Vocabulary** What does **Congress** do?

2. Where are the rules for our government written?

3. Draw a chart to compare the roles of a mayor, a governor, and a President.

Signs of Citizen Pride

Big Idea
Americans show their patriotism in many ways.

Vocabulary

patriotism

patriotic symbol

anthem

peace

The feeling of pride people have for their country is called **patriotism**. People show their patriotism by what they say and do.

Respect the Flag

American citizens show respect for their flag because it is a symbol of their country. A **patriotic symbol** is a picture or object that stands for the ideas the people of a country believe in.

Florida

States have flags, too.

New Mexico

Nevada

Pledge Allegiance

When you say the Pledge of Allegiance, you promise to be true to the flag and to our country.

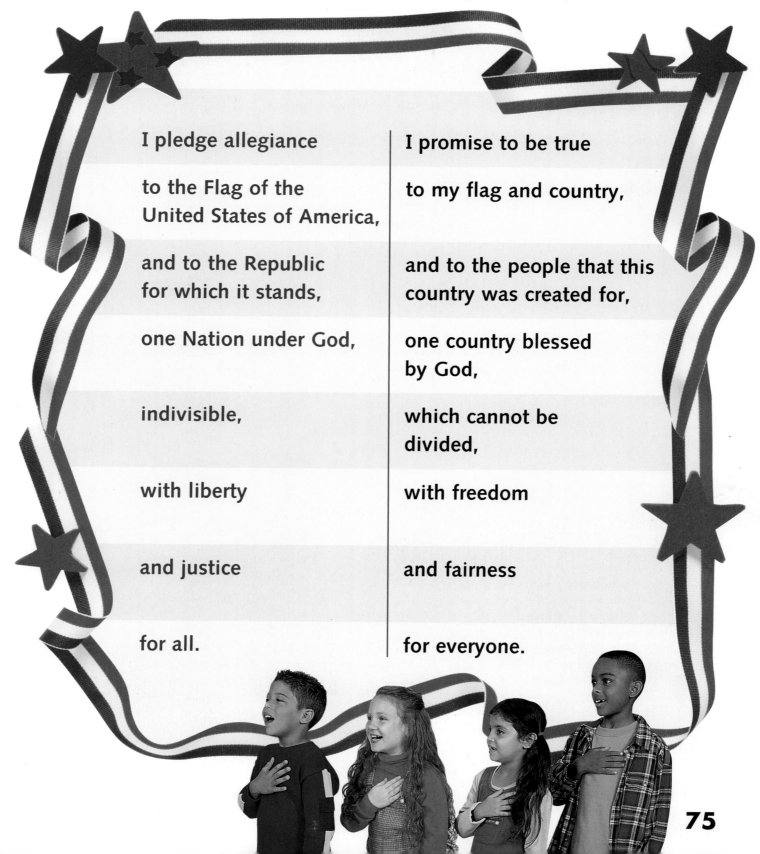

I pledge allegiance	I promise to be true
to the Flag of the United States of America,	to my flag and country,
and to the Republic for which it stands,	and to the people that this country was created for,
one Nation under God,	one country blessed by God,
indivisible,	which cannot be divided,
with liberty	with freedom
and justice	and fairness
for all.	for everyone.

Sing Songs

An **anthem** is the official song of a country. The anthem of the United States of America is "The Star-Spangled Banner." It is about our country's flag.

The Star-Spangled Banner

Oh, say, can you see,
by the dawn's early light,
What so proudly we hailed
at the twilight's last gleaming,
Whose broad stripes and bright
stars, through the perilous fight,
O'er the ramparts we watched,
were so gallantly streaming?
And the rockets' red glare,
the bombs bursting in air,
Gave proof through the night
that our flag was still there.
Oh, say, does that star-spangled
banner yet wave,
O'er the land of the free and
the home of the brave?

Francis Scott Key   1779–1843
Character Trait: Patriotism

Francis Scott Key wrote the words for our country's anthem. He wrote them as a poem during the War of 1812 between the United States and Britain. The flag that he wrote about flew over Fort McHenry in Baltimore. Key was there when the British attacked the fort all night. The next morning he saw that "our flag was still there." Key's poem was later set to music, and in 1931 it became our country's anthem.

MULTIMEDIA BIOGRAPHIES
Visit The Learning Site at
www.harcourtschool.com
to learn about other famous people.

GO
ONLINE

People often stand and sing the national anthem at the start of sports events. Americans sing other patriotic songs at special times, too.

Know Patriotic Symbols

The bald eagle is a powerful American symbol. Watching it fly high up in the sky reminds us of the courage and strength of American citizens. As the national bird, the bald eagle is protected by law.

Uncle Sam is another popular symbol. His initials are U.S. Dressed in the colors of the flag, Uncle Sam is often seen on patriotic posters and in cartoons about the government.

The rose is our national flower. It is a symbol of peace. **Peace** means getting along with other people.

The rose is a beautiful flower with a wonderful smell. But it does have thorns to protect it!

Georgia
Cherokee Rose

Oregon
Oregon Grape

Mississippi
and Louisiana
magnolia

Celebrate Holidays

Flag Day

The idea of celebrating the flag's birthday may have started with a teacher and her class in Fredonia, Wisconsin. In 1949 Congress made June 14 National Flag Day.

Independence Day

On July 4, 1776, American leaders agreed to a Declaration of Independence. They would no longer be ruled by the king of England. Each year on this day, Americans remember how our country began.

Presidents' Day

Two of our most famous Presidents, George Washington and Abraham Lincoln, were born in the month of February. Now we honor all our Presidents on the third Monday of that month.

LESSON 6
Review

1. **Vocabulary** How do Americans show their **patriotism**?

2. What are your state symbols?

3. Choose a patriotic symbol or holiday. Write a poem about how it shows Americans' love of freedom.

Use a Picture Graph

Vocabulary

picture graph

▶ Why It Matters

Some information is easier to find and understand on a chart or graph.

▶ What You Need to Know

A **picture graph** uses pictures to show numbers of things.

In the graph on the next page, the pictures tell you how many states have chosen each bird as their state symbol.

▶ Practice the Skill

Study the picture graph of state birds.

1 How many kinds of birds are shown?

2 Which bird is the symbol of the most states?

3 How many states have chosen the mockingbird?

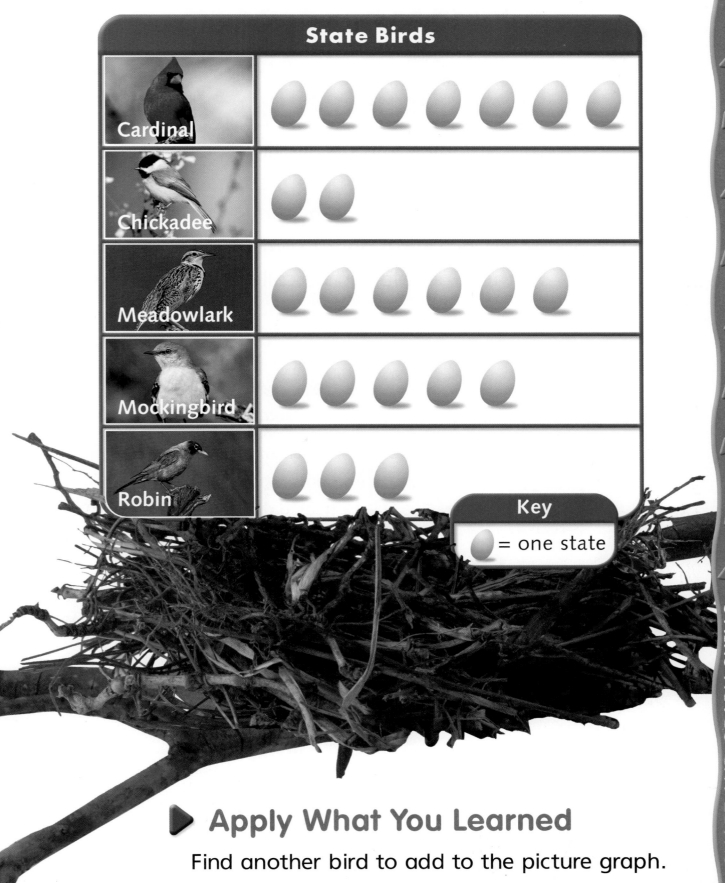

State Birds

Cardinal	🥚🥚🥚🥚🥚🥚🥚
Chickadee	🥚🥚
Meadowlark	🥚🥚🥚🥚🥚🥚
Mockingbird	🥚🥚🥚🥚🥚
Robin	🥚🥚🥚

Key

🥚 = one state

▶ Apply What You Learned

Find another bird to add to the picture graph.

What Makes a Good Citizen

Big Idea

We can learn from people who have been good citizens.

Imagine you are visiting a Good Citizens' Hall of Fame. Whose pictures might you see? There are many ways to be a good citizen. Read about some of the reasons these people can be called good citizens.

Jackie Robinson
1919–1972
Character Trait: Individualism

Jackie Robinson grew up knowing how people were treated differently because of the color of their skin. He worked hard, went to college, served in the Army, and played major league baseball. After baseball, Jackie Robinson helped other African Americans find their dreams.

"A life is not important except in the impact it has on other lives."

Paul Revere
1735–1818
Character Trait: Patriotism

Paul Revere lived in Massachusetts when our country belonged to Great Britain. He thought Americans should be free to make their own laws. Paul Revere was willing to risk his life for freedom. He rode to warn people that British soldiers were coming.

"The British are coming, the British are coming!"

Sojourner Truth
1797?–1883
Character Trait: Honesty

Sojourner Truth was first named Isabella Van Wagener. She took a new name because she felt it was her job to travel and tell the truth. She talked about her past as a slave. Slaves were owned by others and made to work hard without pay. Sojourner Truth spoke against slavery because she believed it was wrong.

"Truth burns up error."

Susan B. Anthony
1820–1906
Character Trait: Fairness

Susan B. Anthony was the first woman shown on American money. She was honored this way because she spoke against unfair laws. In her lifetime only men could vote. Her work helped change laws so that women could vote, too.

"Independence is happiness."

83

Clara Barton
1821–1912
Character Trait: Responsibility

Clara Barton worked all her life to help people. When she was 11 years old, she cared for her sick brother. Years later, during a war, she cared for hurt soldiers. They called her "Angel of the Battlefield." She also started the American branch of the Red Cross. The Red Cross helps people in many ways, for example after natural disasters.

". . .while our soldiers can stand and fight, I can stand and feed and nurse them."

Helen Keller
1880–1968
Character Trait: Courage

Before her second birthday, Helen Keller became ill and lost her sight and hearing. With the help of her teacher, Anne Sullivan, she learned to speak and write. She told others about the hard work it took to find her way. Helen Keller spoke and wrote books to help others. She is often called the First Lady of Courage.

"Life is either a daring adventure or nothing at all."

Mother Teresa
1910–1997
Character Trait: Kindness

Mother Teresa spent her life caring for the poorest people in India and other places. Working with her helpers, Mother Teresa provided food, clothing, and shelter for the "unwanted, unloved, and uncared for." She won the Nobel Peace Prize for her good works. She was also made an honorary citizen of the United States.

"Intense love does not measure. It just gives."

Cesar Chavez
1927–1993
Character Trait: Perseverance

Cesar Chavez and his family were farm workers in California. They moved from farm to farm to pick fruits and vegetables. When Cesar Chavez grew up, he talked to people about **justice**, or fairness, for poor farm workers. He helped the workers get together to ask for more pay and better places to live.

"The fight is never about grapes or lettuce. It is always about people."

Condoleezza Rice
born in 1954
**Character Trait:
Cooperation**

Growing up with parents who were teachers inspired Condoleezza Rice to work hard in school. She was an outstanding student. Now she advises the President about getting along with other countries around the world. She knows how important it is for people to work together.

Yo-Yo Ma
born in 1955
**Character Trait:
Self-discipline**

Yo-Yo Ma was born in Paris, France. He began to play the cello when he was 4 years old. At 19 he was already a great musician. He still works very hard to play difficult music. He also takes time to teach music around the world. He believes that everyone everywhere can share his love of music.

Pedro José Greer, Jr.
born in 1956
**Character Trait:
Trustworthiness**

As a young doctor, Pedro Greer treated people on the streets of Miami. They called him "Joe." He started a walk-in clinic to help the homeless. Since then Dr. Greer has written a book, advised two Presidents, and received many awards for his **public service**. Today he and his clinics continue to help those in need.

Some community workers are trained to take care of people who are hurt or in danger. Police officers, firefighters, and other rescue workers do dangerous jobs to help others.

President Bush thanks rescue workers for their help after the attack on the World Trade Center on September 11, 2001.

Set a good example.

LESSON 7
Review

❶ **Vocabulary** Why is **justice** for all important?

❷ What are some traits of good citizens?

❸ Think of a good citizen in your community. Write about the qualities that make him or her a good citizen.

Find Fact or Opinion

Vocabulary
fact
opinion

▶ Why It Matters

People need to decide whether what they read or hear is true.

▶ What You Need to Know

A **fact** is something that can be proved. An **opinion** is an idea that a person believes to be true but cannot prove.

▶ Practice the Skill

Read the article on the next page. Find two facts and two opinions.

Work on New School Begins

   Workers have started work on the new Mark Twain Elementary School. Mark Twain was one of our country's most popular writers. His real name was Samuel Clemens, and he was born in Florida, Missouri, in 1835. As a young man he was a boat pilot on the beautiful Mississippi River. Later he wrote his best book, <u>The Adventures of Tom Sawyer</u>. Some people think that Tom Sawyer was really Mark Twain. Perhaps our new school should be named for Tom Sawyer!

▶ Apply What You Learned

   Write a paragraph about a famous American. Give both facts and opinions about the person you choose.

An Eagle Care Center

Get Ready

The national bird of the United States is the American bald eagle. For some time, this bird was endangered. This means there were not many left. Thanks to special workers, there are now more bald eagles. At an eagle care center in Oklahoma, workers collect eggs, hatch them, and care for the young eagles. Then they set them free.

Locate It
United States

Oklahoma

What to See

A worker climbs a tree to collect eggs from an eagle's nest. He puts the eggs into a soft travel case to keep them from breaking.

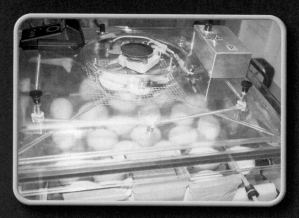

At the center, an incubator keeps the eggs warm.

An eaglet, or baby eagle, breaks through the shell of its egg with its beak.

Workers tag an eagle so they can identify it later.

A bald eagle does not get its white head and tail until it is four years old.

Take a Field Trip

GO ONLINE

A VIRTUAL TOUR
Visit The Learning Site at **www.harcourtschool.com** to take virtual tours of other places of interest in the United States.

READING RAINBOW

A VIDEO TOUR
Check your media center or classroom library for a video featuring a segment from Reading Rainbow.

Focus Skill Prior Knowledge

Finish the K-W-L chart. List what you learned about your community, state, and country.

K-W-L Chart

What I Know	What I Want to Know	What I Learned
1. Our community has a mayor.	1. Who makes the laws?	1.
2. George Washington was our country's first President.	2. What is a constitution?	2.
	3.	3.
	4.	4.
	5.	5.

THINK & WRITE

Choose a Good Citizen
Think about a citizen you admire. What do you know about the person?

Write a Biography
Write a short biography describing the person you admire. Include facts and opinions.

Use Vocabulary

Match the word with its meaning.

1 money paid to the government that is used to pay for services

2 a rule that people in a community must follow

3 a feeling of pride people have for their country

4 the group of citizens that runs a community, state, or country

5 a choice that gets counted

government
(p. 47)
law
(p. 48)
tax
(p. 56)
vote
(p. 60)
patriotism
(p. 74)

Recall Facts

6 How do Americans choose their leaders?

7 How are a mayor, a governor, and the President alike? How are they different?

8 Name and describe two symbols of our country.

9 How many parts does our country's government have?

    A 1   **C** 2

    B 3   **D** 4

10 Which of these is a government service?

    F pet care   **H** public schools

    G car repair   **J** haircuts

Think Critically

11 How do Americans show their patriotism on holidays?

12 What are some traits of a good citizen?

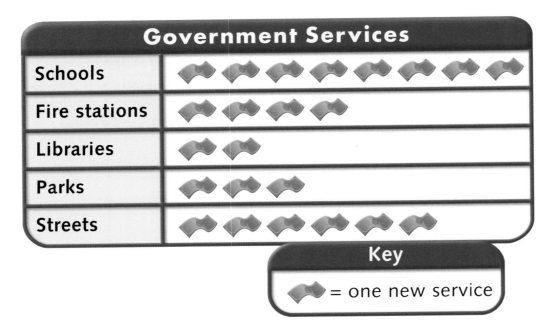

Government Services	
Schools	🪶🪶🪶🪶🪶🪶🪶🪶
Fire stations	🪶🪶🪶🪶
Libraries	🪶🪶
Parks	🪶🪶🪶
Streets	🪶🪶🪶🪶🪶🪶

Key

🪶 = one new service

13 What symbol is used for new services?

14 How many new schools were built?

15 Which service had the fewest new additions?

16 How many more fire stations than parks were built?

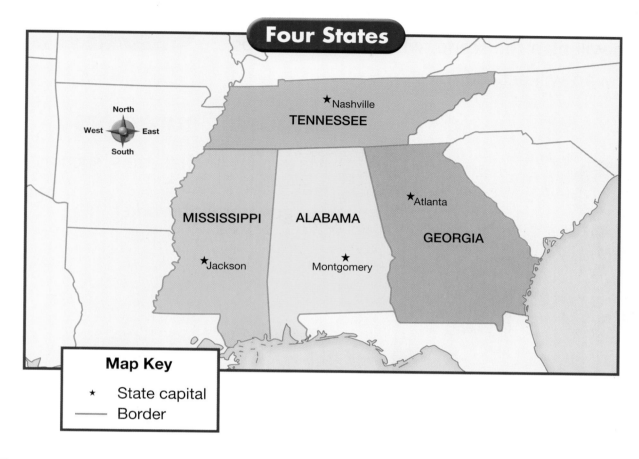

Four States

North
West — East
South

★Nashville
TENNESSEE

★Atlanta

MISSISSIPPI   **ALABAMA**

GEORGIA

★Jackson   ★
        Montgomery

Map Key
★   State capital
—   Border

17 What city is the capital of Georgia?

18 Of which state is Montgomery the capital?

19 Which two states shown share borders with Mississippi?

20 If you traveled from Atlanta to Nashville, which border would you cross?

Unit Activities

GO ONLINE

Visit The Learning Site at **www.harcourtschool.com** for additional activities.

Complete the Unit Project Work with a group to role-play citizenship scenes. Decide who will plan the scene, who will make props, and who will act the roles.

Choose Characters

Make a list of characters, such as
- a public servant
- a government worker
- a community helper
- a famous patriot

Perform the Scenes

Role-play your scenes. Invite audience members to ask you questions. Answer them as your character. Take turns acting different roles.

Visit Your Library

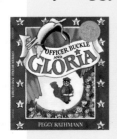

Officer Buckle and Gloria by Peggy Rathmann. Officer Buckle and his police dog, Gloria, share safety tips.

Amelia Bedelia 4 Mayor by Herman Parish. Amelia is persuaded to run for public office.

Celebrate the 50 States! by Loreen Leedy. Find out about each of the fifty states and Washington, D.C.

Looking at the Earth

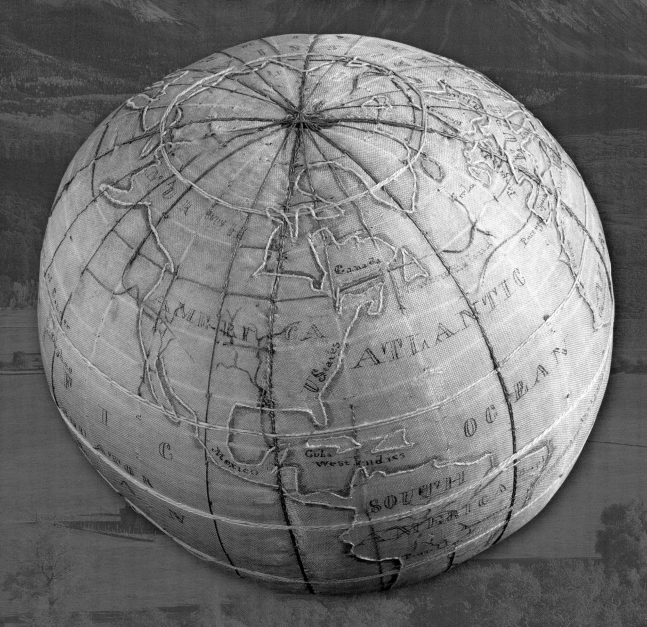

A silk globe sewn
by a schoolgirl, 1814

3

Looking at the Earth

" Oh, I'm all for rockets
And worlds cold or hot,
But I'm wild in love
With the planet we've got! "

—Frances Frost,
from "Valentine for Earth" in <u>The Little Naturalist</u>, 1959

(Focus Skill) Categorize

As you read this unit, do the following.

- Make a web to show what you learn about the geography of Earth.
- Group ideas under landforms, bodies of water, resources, and conservation.

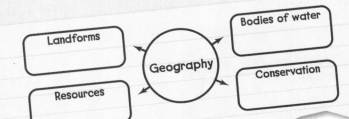

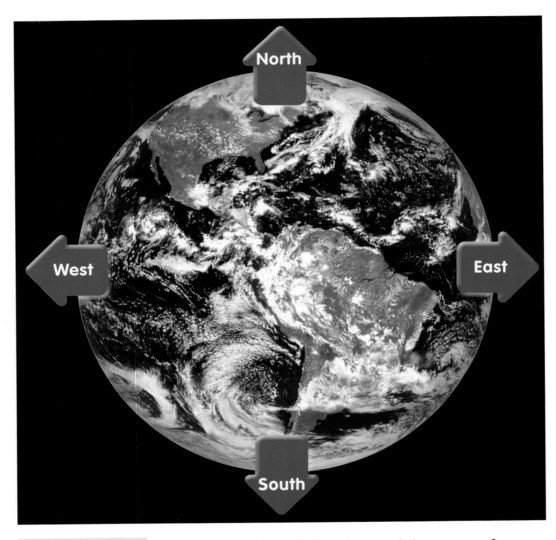

geography   The study of Earth and its people. (page 100)

cardinal directions   The main directions of north, south, east, and west. (page 124)

landform A kind of land with a special shape, such as a mountain, hill, or plain. (page 112)

conservation Working to save resources or make them last longer. (page 148)

natural resource Something found in nature that people can use to meet their needs. (page 128)

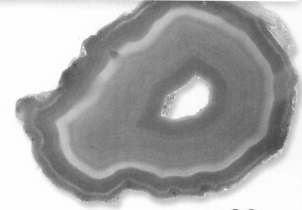

TULIP SEES AMERICA

by Cynthia Rylant
illustrated by Lisa Desimini

Find out what a boy and his dog
learn about **geography** as they
travel across the country.

When I was a boy, I didn't see much of America.
My parents were homebodies, so I stayed home.

But when I grew up, I knew I was different.
I wanted to see America.

So I bought a little green Beetle
and in it I put a small box of clothes,
a small bag of food, and my dog, Tulip.

And we left Ohio
and went
across America.

This is what we saw:

The farms in Iowa. They are pictures:
White houses. Red roofs.
Green, green rolling hills
and black garden soil all around them.

Farms like castles in a fairyland,
serene in the morning fog.

There are no farms like Iowa's.

The skies in Nebraska.
They are everything.
They are vast and dark
and low and ominous.
And a tiny Beetle feels even tinier,
driving beneath them.

It feels a little afraid.

Then the skies break open
into blue and white and
yellow and pink,
and it is like one great long breath
of freedom and air.

There are no skies like Nebraska's.

The wind in Wyoming.
Everything flaps.

Tulip's ears flapped
all the way across Wyoming.
And when we stopped to
get out of the Beetle,
the wind filled our noses
and watered our eyes
and Tulip was ready to get
back into the car.

There is no wind like Wyoming's.

105

The mountains in Colorado.
They are all rock.
Piles of rock as high as the sky
and a river running under them.
Tulip saw a ram on the rocks
and barked for half an hour.
She barked all over those mountains.
At elk. At wolves. At deer.

Our little Beetle puffed like an old man,
driving up and up.

There are no mountains like Colorado's.

The desert in Nevada.
There is no place to hide in a desert,
and you are glad you are not a rabbit
or a mouse someone might want to eat.
The desert runs so far and so wide that
you think if you are there too long,
you will go crazy.

Its flowers are strange and beautiful,
and Tulip chased salamanders between its rocks.

There is no desert like Nevada's.

The ocean in Oregon.
You drive up a winding mountain road
and you think there is no ocean anywhere.
You drive between a stand of firs
and you think: no ocean.

Then you blink,
and there it is:

You are on a cliff and
the water is below you
and as far as you can see,
and you think the earth
has dropped away from
you and you'd better know
how to swim.

Tulip could not stop running.
Tulip is an ocean dog.

There is no ocean like
Oregon's.

And this is where we stayed.

Think About It

1 How are Iowa and Nevada different?

2 Find and write two more facts about one of the states Tulip visited.

Read a Book

Start the Unit Project

A Landscape Mural Your class will draw a mural to show how people live on different kinds of land. As you read this unit, remember the different kinds of land, weather, and resources.

Use Technology

Visit The Learning Site at **www.harcourtschool.com** for additional activities, primary sources, and other resources to use in this unit.

Our Country's Land

Big Idea
The land in our country has many shapes and sizes.

Vocabulary
landform
hill
plain
mountain
valley
island
peninsula

As Tulip traveled from Ohio to Oregon, she saw many kinds of landforms. A **landform** is a kind of land with a special shape.

Hills and Plains

Some parts of Iowa are covered by rolling hills. A **hill** is land that rises above the land around it.

hill

Locate It
United States

Iowa

plain

Locate It
United States

Nebraska

The Nebraska **plain**, or flat land, stretches as far as the eye can see. The plains of Nebraska are part of the Great Plains, which spread from Texas to Montana. Many farms and cities have grown up on the plains in the middle of our country.

Mountains and Valleys

Snow never melts on top of some of the highest mountains of Colorado. A **mountain** is a very high hill.

Between the high mountains are valleys. A **valley** is low land between hills or mountains. It often has a stream or river flowing through it.

Locate It
United States

Colorado

mountain

valley

Islands and Peninsulas

Small and large islands are found in bodies of water. An **island** is a landform with water all around it. Some islands are connected to land by bridges. Others can be reached only by boat or plane. The state of Hawaii is made up of many islands.

Hawaiian island

If a landform is surrounded on only three sides by water, it is called a **peninsula**. The state of Florida is a large peninsula. The photograph shows how Florida looks from space.

Florida peninsula

**LESSON 1
Review**

(Focus Skill) ❶ **Categorize** What are two kinds of land?

❷ **Vocabulary** What **landforms** do you live on or near?

❸ Draw or cut out pictures to make a picture dictionary of landforms.

Our Country's Water

Big Idea
Rivers and lakes are important to all parts of our country.

Vocabulary
river
lake
gulf

Like landforms, the bodies of water in our country have many shapes and sizes. The United States lies between two great oceans, the Atlantic and the Pacific. There are also bodies of water all over the land.

Rivers

A **river** is a stream of water that flows across the land. The longest river in the United States is the Mississippi River. It flows down the middle of our country from Minnesota to Louisiana.

Mississippi River

Lake Itasca

The Mississippi River starts at Lake Itasca in Minnesota. A **lake** is a low spot on the land that has filled with water. Water flows out of Lake Itasca and forms the Mississippi River.

FAST FACT Did you know that you can walk across the Mississippi River at Lake Itasca? There it begins as a narrow, shallow stream. Near the Gulf of Mexico, the Mississippi River is more than three miles wide.

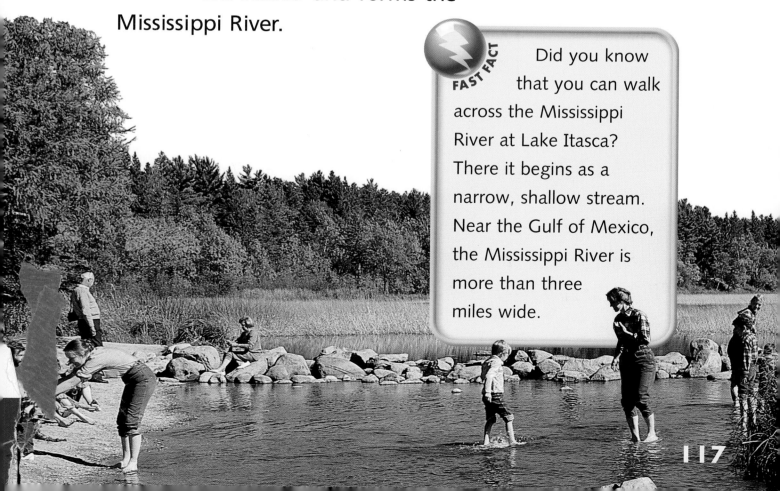

The Gulf of Mexico

The Mississippi River ends in Louisiana, where it flows into the Gulf of Mexico. A **gulf** is a large body of ocean water that is partly surrounded by land. Five states are on the Gulf of Mexico. They are Texas, Louisiana, Mississippi, Alabama, and Florida. The country of Mexico also lies on the Gulf.

Gulf States

Mississippi

Alabama

Texas

Louisiana

Florida

North

West — East

South

MEXICO

Gulf of Mexico

Gulf of Mexico in Florida

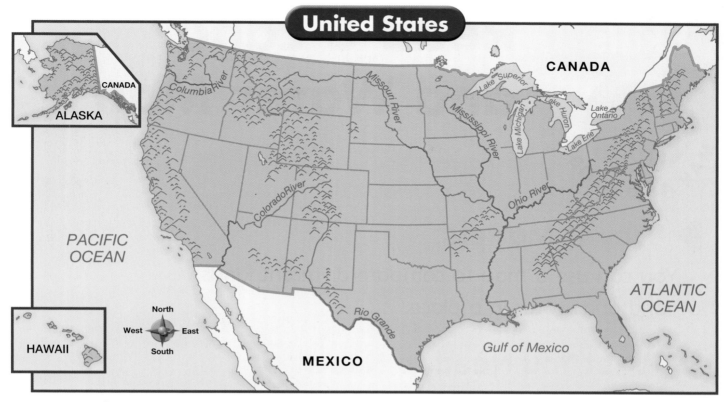

United States

CANADA
ALASKA

PACIFIC
OCEAN

HAWAII

North
West — East
South

MEXICO

CANADA

Columbia River

Missouri River

Mississippi River

Lake Superior

Lake Michigan

Lake Huron

Lake Ontario

Lake Erie

Ohio River

Colorado River

Rio Grande

ATLANTIC
OCEAN

Gulf of Mexico

GEOGRAPHY THEME

Where are the Great Lakes?

The Great Lakes

The Mississippi River is one of many rivers in our country. There are also many lakes. The largest of these are called the Great Lakes because of their size. They are Lakes Superior, Michigan, Huron, Erie, and Ontario.

LESSON 2
Review

1 **Vocabulary** How is a **lake** different from a **gulf**?

2 Where does the Mississippi River begin and end?

3 Make a list of the rivers in your state.

Read a Land and Water Map

▶ Why It Matters

You can use a map to compare different kinds of land and water in a place.

▶ What You Need to Know

A map uses colors, symbols, and labels to show different kinds of land. Blue shows water. Labels tell the names of the kinds of land and water.

Orange shows deserts.

Yellow shows hills.

Purple shows mountains.

Green shows plains.

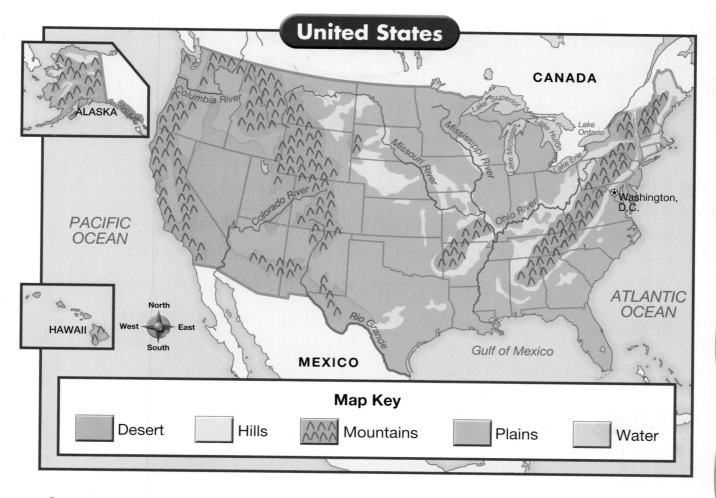

United States

CANADA

ALASKA

PACIFIC OCEAN

HAWAII

North
West   East
South

MEXICO

Columbia River

Missouri River

Mississippi River

Lake Superior

Lake Michigan

Lake Huron

Lake Ontario

Lake Erie

Colorado River

Rio Grande

Ohio River

⊛Washington, D.C.

ATLANTIC OCEAN

Gulf of Mexico

Map Key

Desert   Hills   ^^^ Mountains   Plains   Water

▶ Practice the Skill

1 Look at the map key. What kinds of land are shown on the map?

2 What kind of land covers most of the United States?

3 On what kind of land is Washington, D.C.?

▶ Apply What You Learned

Find the outline of your state on the map. Use the key to describe the land and bodies of water.

Practice your map and globe skills with the **GeoSkills CD-ROM**.

Maps and Globes

Big Idea
Maps and globes help us locate places on Earth.

Vocabulary

continent

globe

cardinal directions

equator

This map of the world shows the seven continents. A **continent** is one of the seven main land areas on Earth. The seven continents are Africa, Antarctica, Asia, Australia, Europe, North America, and South America.

The World

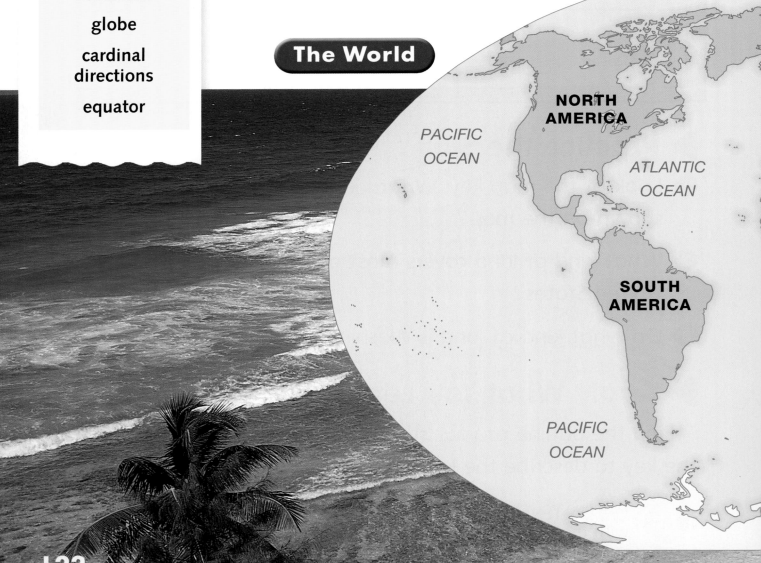

NORTH AMERICA

PACIFIC OCEAN

ATLANTIC OCEAN

SOUTH AMERICA

PACIFIC OCEAN

This map also shows that much of the world is covered by oceans. The four large oceans are the Pacific Ocean, the Atlantic Ocean, the Indian Ocean, and the Arctic Ocean.

GEOGRAPHY THEME

What ocean lies between Africa and Australia?

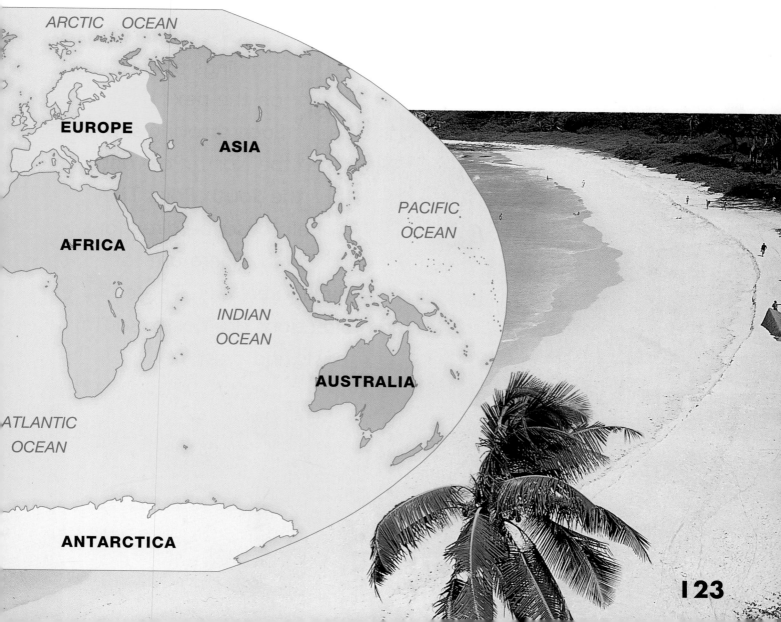

ARCTIC OCEAN

EUROPE

ASIA

AFRICA

PACIFIC OCEAN

INDIAN OCEAN

AUSTRALIA

ATLANTIC OCEAN

ANTARCTICA

A map does not always show the true shape of Earth or the true size of the continents and oceans. That is because maps are flat, and Earth is round. A **globe** is a better model of Earth because it is round, too. However, a map is easier to carry with you.

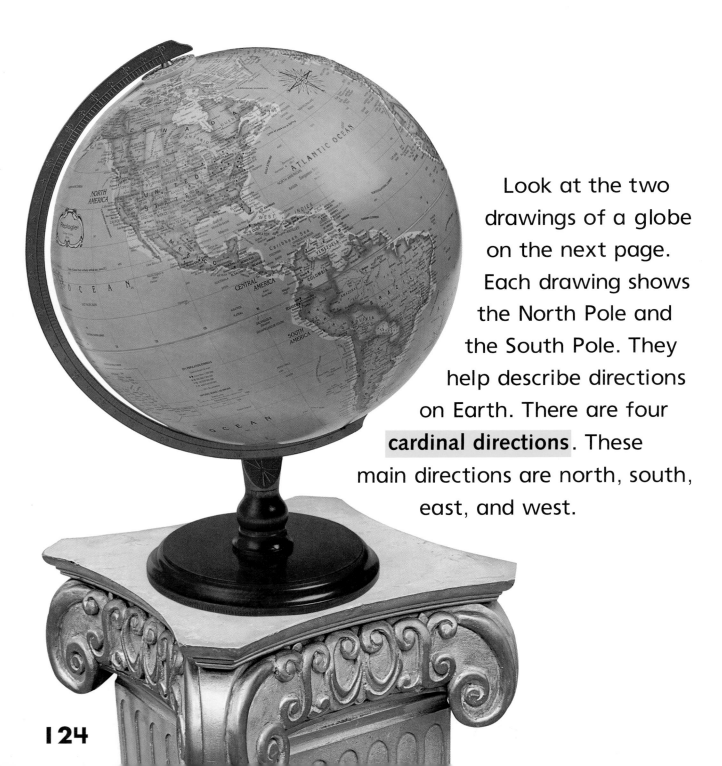

Look at the two drawings of a globe on the next page. Each drawing shows the North Pole and the South Pole. They help describe directions on Earth. There are four **cardinal directions**. These main directions are north, south, east, and west.

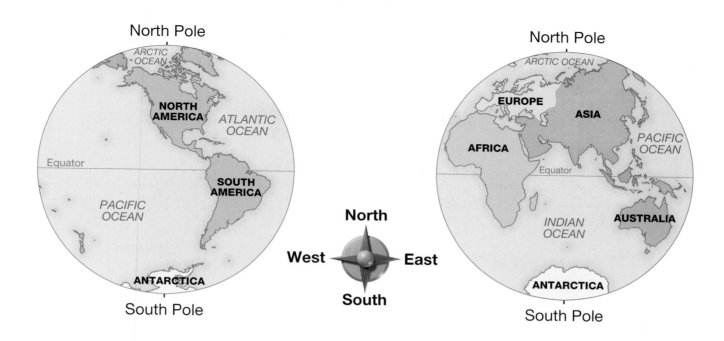

North Pole

ARCTIC OCEAN

NORTH AMERICA

ATLANTIC OCEAN

Equator

SOUTH AMERICA

PACIFIC OCEAN

ANTARCTICA

South Pole

North Pole

ARCTIC OCEAN

EUROPE

ASIA

AFRICA

PACIFIC OCEAN

Equator

INDIAN OCEAN

AUSTRALIA

ANTARCTICA

South Pole

North

West   East

South

South is the direction toward the South Pole. North is toward the North Pole. When you face north, east is to your right. West is to your left.

Put your finger on the line drawn halfway between the two poles. This is the equator. The **equator** is an imaginary line that divides Earth in half. Places on Earth can be described as north of the equator or south of the equator.

LESSON 3 Review

Focus Skill ❶ **Categorize**   How is a globe different from a map?

❷ **Vocabulary**   Name the seven **continents**.

❸ Pick a continent. Use the cardinal directions to describe where it is located on a globe.

Find Directions on a Map

Vocabulary

compass rose

▶ Why It Matters

Knowing cardinal directions can help you get from one place to another. These direction words help you describe where places are.

▶ What You Need to Know

A **compass rose** gives the cardinal directions on a map. <u>N</u> stands for north, <u>S</u> for south, <u>E</u> for east, and <u>W</u> for west.

▶ Practice the Skill

❶ Which state is east of Oregon?

❷ In which direction would you go from New Mexico to Colorado?

❸ Which state is west of Nevada?

❹ In which direction would you go from Georgia to Florida?

United States

MONTANA
NORTH DAKOTA
MINNESOTA
CANADA
NEW HAMPSHIRE
MAINE
VERMONT
Lake Superior
MICHIGAN
Lake Huron
Lake Ontario
NEW YORK
MASSACHUSETTS
RHODE ISLAND
IDAHO
WYOMING
SOUTH DAKOTA
WISCONSIN
Lake Michigan
Lake Erie
PENNSYLVANIA
CONNECTICUT
NEBRASKA
IOWA
INDIANA
OHIO
NEW JERSEY
DELAWARE
UTAH
COLORADO
ILLINOIS
WEST VIRGINIA
MARYLAND
WASHINGTON, D.C.
ARIZONA
KANSAS
MISSOURI
KENTUCKY
VIRGINIA
NEW MEXICO
OKLAHOMA
ARKANSAS
TENNESSEE
NORTH CAROLINA
SOUTH CAROLINA
ATLANTIC OCEAN
TEXAS
ALABAMA
MISSISSIPPI
GEORGIA
LOUISIANA
MEXICO
North
West   East
South
Gulf of Mexico
FLORIDA

Map Key
⊛ National capital
— Border

▶ Apply What You Learned

With a classmate, identify some places in your classroom, school, or neighborhood. Use cardinal directions to describe how to get to them from where you are.

Practice your map and globe skills with the **GeoSkills CD-ROM**.

4

Using Natural Resources

Big Idea
People use natural resources to meet their needs.

A **natural resource** is something found in nature that people can use. Water, air, trees, and soil are natural resources. People use natural resources to help meet their needs for food, clothing, and shelter.

air

water

wood

soil

Parker Dam on the Colorado River

People Use Water

People use water for many things. They use it for drinking, cooking, bathing, washing clothes, and cleaning. They use it for growing plants. They use it when they ride in boats and ships.

People also use water to make electricity. They build dams on rivers. Inside the dam, the flow of the river turns big machines that make electricity.

129

People Use Air

Air is another important natural resource. People and plants need clean air to live. Like water, air can also be used to make electricity.

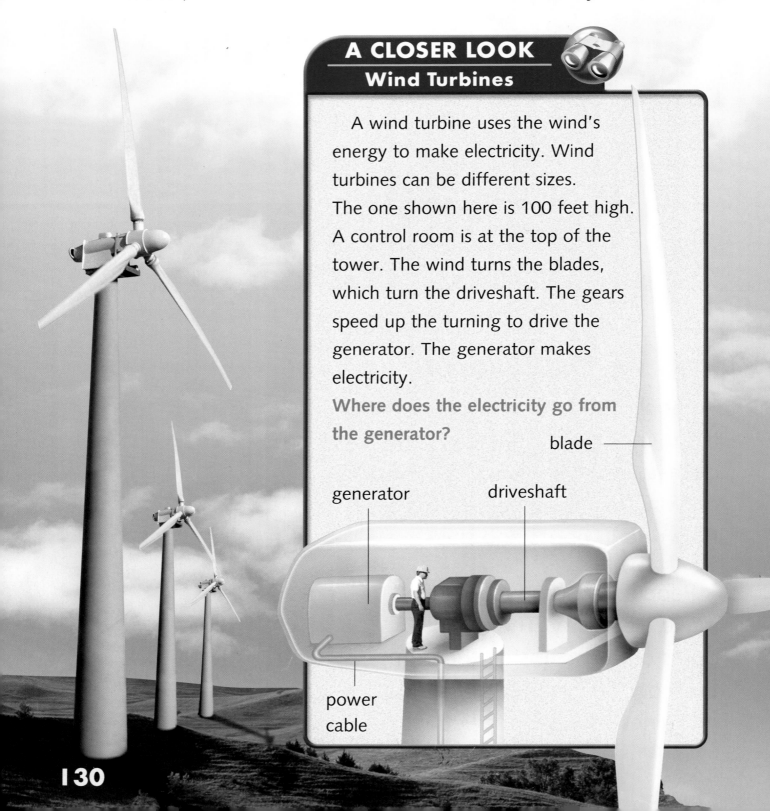

A CLOSER LOOK
Wind Turbines

A wind turbine uses the wind's energy to make electricity. Wind turbines can be different sizes. The one shown here is 100 feet high. A control room is at the top of the tower. The wind turns the blades, which turn the driveshaft. The gears speed up the turning to drive the generator. The generator makes electricity.

Where does the electricity go from the generator?

blade

generator

driveshaft

power cable

People Use Trees

Trees are a resource that people use to make many things. They use wood from trees to make furniture and to build homes. People also use wood to make paper.

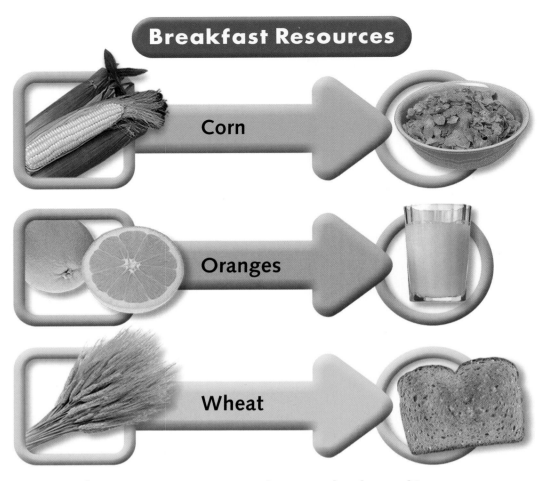

Breakfast Resources

Corn →

Oranges →

Wheat →

What resource is used to make bread?

People Use Soil

People use soil to grow crops. A **crop** is a plant people grow for food or other needs. Wheat is a crop that people use to make bread and pasta to eat. Cotton is a crop that people use to make cloth for clothing.

Corn is another plant that people grow as a crop. Much of the corn is used to feed farm animals. Animals such as sheep and cows are raised to provide wool and milk.

Farming is an important job. Farmers must know how to keep the soil healthy. They learn how and when to plant and how weather affects their crops. People have been learning to become better farmers for thousands of years.

George Washington Carver
1864–1943
Character Trait: Inventiveness

For a long time, many farmers in some states grew only cotton. This made the soil poor. Then the cotton would not grow. George Washington Carver showed farmers that planting peanuts and sweet potatoes made the soil rich again.

MULTIMEDIA BIOGRAPHIES
Visit The Learning Site at
www.harcourtschool.com
to learn about other famous people.

GO ONLINE

LESSON 4
Review

❶ **Vocabulary** Name two **natural resources** and tell how they are used.

❷ How does soil help meet our need for food?

❸ Keep a log or journal for one day. Write down the different kinds of natural resources you use.

Read a Table

Vocabulary

table

▶ Why It Matters

A **table** is a chart used to organize information. Knowing how to read a table can help you easily understand and compare information.

▶ What You Need to Know

The title of a table tells you what it shows. Columns on a table go up and down. Rows go across. To read a table, you must follow a column down and a row across to see where they meet. The labels at the top of each column and beside each row explain what you are seeing.

▶ Practice the Skill

❶ What does the table show?

❷ What resources are listed in the table?

❸ Name two ways people use sunflowers.

❹ Which resource is used to make tools?

How People Use Resources

Natural Resources	Ways People Use Natural Resources			
Trees	fruits/nuts	firewood	lumber	paper
Sunflowers	cooking oil	birdseed	soap	paint
Iron	steel beams	paper clips	bicycle	tools
Oil	plastic toys	medicines	candles	fuel

▶ Apply What You Learned

Make a table showing how you use water at home, at school, and in the community.

CHART AND GRAPH SKILLS

Primary Sources

Better Tools

Many of the tools we use today to meet our needs are different from the ones people used long ago. Technology has made our lives easier. **Technology** is the use of new inventions in everyday life.

1 What do these tools tell you about farming long ago?

seed planter

scythe

wooden plow

2 What do these pictures tell you about how plowing has changed?

horse-drawn plow

early tractor

modern tractor

3 What do these tools tell you about farming today?

disc

seed planter

cultivator

harvester

Activity

Write a paragraph to tell how better tools have made people's lives easier.

Research

Visit The Learning Site at
www.harcourtschool.com
to research other primary sources.

5 People and the Land

Big Idea
People affect the places they live, and the places affect the people.

Vocabulary
forest

fuel

climate

tornado

blizzard

People live in all kinds of places on Earth. They choose a place that has the land, the water, and the natural resources they need.

Northern Georgia

Long ago only forest covered the area where Chickamauga, Georgia, now stands. A **forest** is a large area of trees. Then farm families came to the valley. They cut down trees to build homes and cleared the land to plant crops. They changed the land as they built a community.

Locate It
United States

Chickamauga, Georgia

Georgia's Natural Resources

Chickamauga was started by people who found coal in the ground nearby. They brought the coal to the town by train. In large ovens the coal was made into coke. The coke was then used as a fuel to make steel and iron. **Fuel** is a resource that can be burned for heat and for power to make machines work.

Coal

Today there is no more coal near Chickamauga. The coke oven workers found different jobs or moved away. The farm families stayed. Many of them still grow crops in Chickamauga's rich soil.

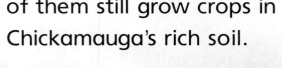

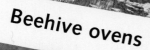

Beehive ovens

Chickamauga market

FAST FACT In the 1800s gold was another important resource in northern Georgia. People came from all over to mine the gold, hoping to become rich.

Roswell, Georgia, grew up near Vickery Creek. The creek's waters provided the power to run cotton mills built by Roswell King. Many people moved there to work at the mills.

Roswell grew and changed. Parts of the mills are still there, but they are not used. Now there are new office buildings and shopping centers among the beautiful old homes and buildings.

Locate It
United States

Roswell, Georgia

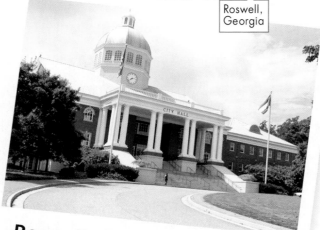

Roswell, Georgia, City Hall

Georgia's Climate

One of the nice things about living in Georgia is the climate. **Climate** is the kind of weather a place has over time. People in Georgia enjoy each of the four seasons. Spring is rainy and mild. Summer is hot. Fall is dry. Winters can be cold and snowy in northern Georgia.

summer

spring

fall

winter

143

Natural Hazards

As in most places, Georgia's weather can be dangerous at times. Tornados can form. A **tornado** is a strong, whirling wind that causes great damage to land and buildings. In winter the wind can blow the snow in a heavy snowstorm called a **blizzard**.

Tornado

• SCIENCE AND TECHNOLOGY •

Predicting Natural Hazards

Weather forecasters help us prepare for bad weather. Technology helps them predict storms. They watch storms forming and draw maps to show where they are.

Chattahoochee River

Flood

When there is too much snow or rain, rivers and streams can flood. Like strong winds, floodwaters damage the land and put people in danger. Most people build their homes away from low places to protect them from floods.

LESSON 5
Review

① **Vocabulary** How does the **climate** where you live affect the people in your community?

② In what ways do people in your community use natural resources?

③ Draw a picture to show ways people have changed the land where you live.

Use a Map Scale

Vocabulary

map scale

▶ Why It Matters

A map shows a place much smaller than it is on Earth. A **map scale** helps you find how far one place really is from another.

▶ What You Need to Know

Step 1 Lay a piece of paper between two places on a map.

Step 2 Mark the paper at each place.

Step 3 Place the marked paper along the map scale with one of the marks at zero. See how far it is to the second mark.

Practice the Skill

1. How many miles are there between Chickamauga and Atlanta?

2. How far is it from Atlanta to Albany?

3. How far is it from Roswell to Macon?

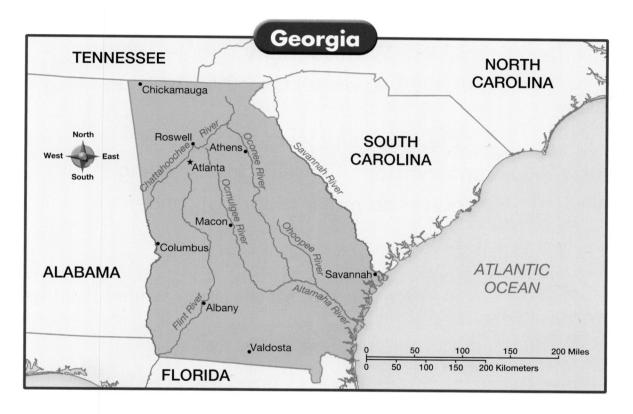

Apply What You Learned

Find a map of your state. Practice using the scale to measure the distance from one place to another.

Practice your map and globe skills with the **GeoSkills CD-ROM**.

Caring for Resources

Big Idea
We can conserve and protect our natural resources.

Vocabulary

conservation

recycle

pollution

There are six billion people in the world. This means that our planet is getting crowded. With so many people, we must find ways to protect Earth's resources.

One way to protect resources is conservation. **Conservation** is saving resources to make them last longer.

We can turn off the water while brushing.

We can write on both sides of paper.

Another way to take care of our resources is to recycle. When you **recycle** something you use it again. Look at how cans, cartons, and boxes can be reused.

I RESPECT MY ENVIRONMENT

Once is not enough...
RECYCLE

Sometimes our natural resources become dirty. This is called **pollution**. If we do not have clean water and air, people, plants, and animals will be hurt.

Garbage can also cause pollution. Communities find ways to remove and store their garbage. Some use it to make new land.

Foster City, California

FAST FACT
Some towns and cities are built on top of landfill. Landfill is garbage that is packed in layers and covered with soil.

Some people use their food garbage to keep their soil healthy. You can help, too. Do not litter.

Save our resources.

LESSON 6
Review

1 **Vocabulary** How does **conservation** protect our resources?

2 What can you do to help recycle?

3 Make a poster showing some ways to protect Earth's resources.

Make a Thoughtful Decision

Vocabulary

decision

▶ Why It Matters

Every day you must make **decisions**. Some choices are simple. For others you must take time to make a wise decision.

▶ What You Need to Know

Step 1 Know you have to make a decision.

Step 2 Gather information.

Step 3 Identify choices.

Step 4 Predict consequences.

Step 5 Take action.

▶ Practice the Skill

We use natural gas to cook with and gas and oil to heat our homes and businesses. We also use gasoline to run our cars and machines. If we use too much fuel, less will be left, and it will cost more. Use the steps for making a thoughtful decision to plan ways to conserve these resources.

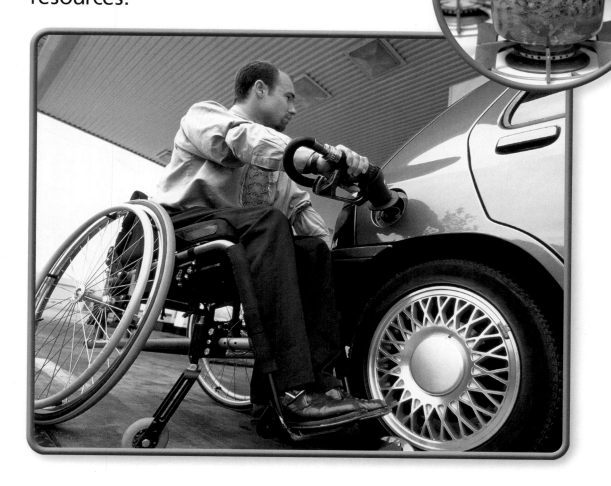

▶ Apply What You Learned

Keep a weekly log of the ways you and your friends help protect resources.

VISIT A POTTER

Some people use earth to create art. Dawn Navasie is a Hopi potter. Visit the pueblo in New Mexico where she lives and works.

Locate It
United States

New Mexico

What to See

First, Dawn mixes two kinds of clay from the earth for her pottery.

Hopis have made their pots in the same way for many years. Dawn coils ropes of clay, one on top of another, to form a pot.

Next, Dawn smoothes the sides of the pot, first with her hands and then with a stone.

Then Dawn makes yucca brushes and mixes paints from natural materials. She uses these to paint designs on her pottery.

Last, Dawn prepares her pot for firing. She protects it from the flames with large pieces of pottery.

The hot fire of juniper wood hardens the pot.

You can see the difference in color between a fired and an unfired pot.

Take a Field Trip

GO ONLINE

A VIRTUAL TOUR
Visit The Learning Site at **www.harcourtschool.com** to take virtual tours of Native American art and craft exhibits.

READING RAINBOW

A VIDEO TOUR
Check your media center or classroom library for a video featuring a segment from Reading Rainbow.

(Focus Skill) Categorize

Use what you have learned to categorize information about our country's geography.

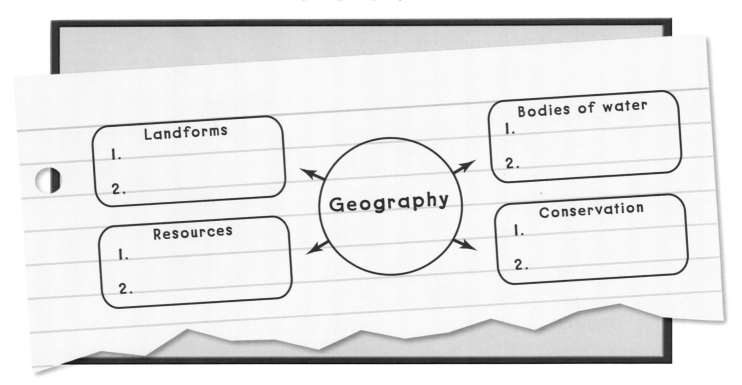

Landforms
1.
2.

Resources
1.
2.

Geography

Bodies of water
1.
2.

Conservation
1.
2.

THINK & WRITE

Make a List   List some adjectives you could use to describe mountains, plains, deserts, forests, and rivers.

Write a Paragraph   Write a paragraph about one of the places. Use your adjectives to describe it.

Use Vocabulary

Choose the best word to finish each sentence.

1 Water is an important _____ that we need to live.

2 A peninsula is a _____ with water on three sides of it.

3 We can protect our resources through _____.

4 People study _____ to understand how people live on Earth.

conservation
(p. 148)
geography
(p. 100)
landform
(p. 112)
natural resource
(p. 128)

Recall Facts

5 Name and describe two kinds of land.

6 How is a map different from a globe?

7 How do people change the land?

8 The Mississippi River flows into—

  A Lake Itasca.   **B** the Gulf of Mexico.

  C the Pacific Ocean.   **D** the Missouri River.

9 Which of the following are natural resources?

  F soil and air   **G** hammer and nails

  H cars and clothes   **J** canned corn and frozen corn

10 Why is it important to study the climate of a place?

11 How can you help protect our natural resources?

Apply Chart and Graph Skills

State Facts		
State	**Big River**	**Main Crops**
Florida	Saint Johns River	oranges, tomatoes, sugarcane
Georgia	Chattahoochee River	peanuts, cotton, soybeans, corn
Mississippi	Mississippi River	cotton, soybeans, corn, hay
New Mexico	Pecos River	hay, chilies, wheat
Oregon	John Day River	wheat, potatoes, barley, pears, raspberries

12 What states are shown on the table?

13 What state has a river by the same name?

14 What crops are grown in New Mexico?

15 Which two states have large fruit crops?

16 Which states grow soybeans?

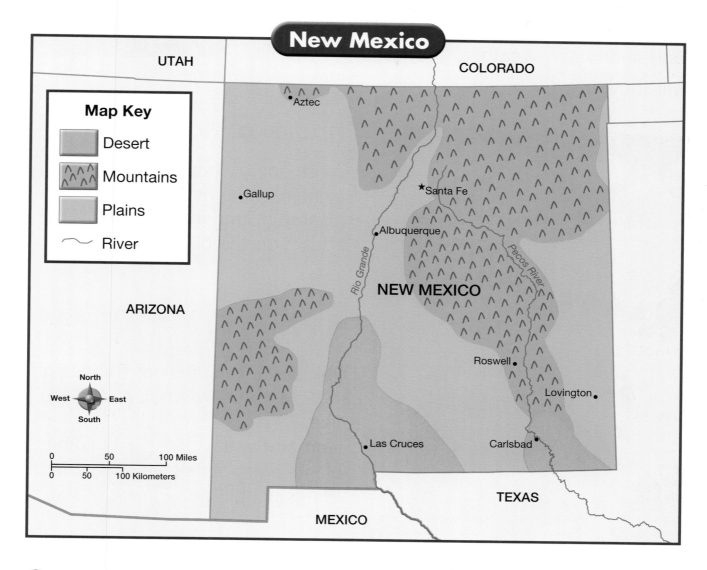

New Mexico

UTAH

COLORADO

Map Key

Desert

Mountains

Plains

River

•Aztec

•Gallup

★Santa Fe

•Albuquerque

NEW MEXICO

ARIZONA

Rio Grande

Pecos River

Roswell•

Lovington•

North

West — East

South

Las Cruces

Carlsbad•

0   50   100 Miles

0   50   100 Kilometers

TEXAS

MEXICO

17 On which kind of landform is Lovington?

18 What river flows to the west of Las Cruces?

19 In which direction from Albuquerque is Santa Fe?

20 How far is Gallup from Aztec?

Unit Activities

Complete the Unit Project Work with your group to finish the unit project. Decide what land and water, weather, and resources you will show in your mural.

GO ONLINE

Visit The Learning Site at **www.harcourtschool.com** for additional activities.

Choose a Place

Choose one of these places to draw.
- a cabin in the mountains
- a campground in the desert
- a farm on the plains

Make a List

Think about the kinds of things you can draw to show what your place is like.
- land and water
- plants and animals
- things people do
- buildings
- weather
- clothing

Visit Your Library

This Land Is Your Land by Woody Guthrie. Beautiful drawings bring this favorite song to life.

Our Big Home: An Earth Poem by Linda Glaser. The verses in this book tell about our home planet.

Are We There Yet, Daddy? by Virginia Walters. A father and son use maps on a long trip to Grandma's house.

Learn About People

A West African
djembe

Unit 4

Learn About People

> ❝If a man does not keep pace with his companions, perhaps it is because he hears a different drummer.❞
>
> —Henry David Thoreau, Walden, 1854

⭐(Focus Skill) Generalize

As you read this unit, do the following.

- List important facts about different groups of people, such as how they live and what they celebrate.
- Use the facts to write a general statement about how these facts help describe different people.

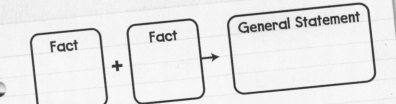

Fact + Fact → General Statement

culture   A people's way of life. (page 169)

heritage   The culture and traditions handed down to people by their ancestors. (page 178)

communication The sharing of ideas and information. (page 196)

ancestor A family member who lived a long time ago. (page 182)

custom A people's way of doing something. (page 186)

ESKIMO GAMES

from Sports Illustrated for Kids

People everywhere enjoy recreation. The Inuit, or Eskimos, have special games they like to play.

Each spring, young athletes from all over Alaska compete in the Native Youth Olympics. The competition is made up of nine events. These events were created thousands of years ago by Eskimos, the native Alaskans.

In the nine events, athletes jump, kick, hop, and tug. Some events are exhausting. Others hurt a little! Eskimos played these games to practice skills they needed to live and to stay in shape and have fun.

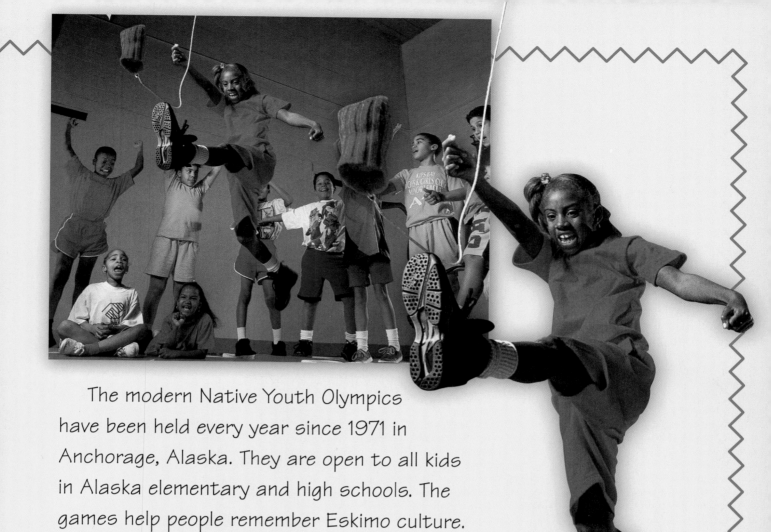

The modern Native Youth Olympics have been held every year since 1971 in Anchorage, Alaska. They are open to all kids in Alaska elementary and high schools. The games help people remember Eskimo culture.

Here are rules and tips for one of the events. Challenge yourself and your friends!

SEAL HOP

In water, seals are graceful swimmers, but on land, they bounce and flop. They wriggle on their bellies and pull themselves along with their front flippers. The seal-hop event copies the way a seal moves on land.

Warning: The seal hop is really tough to do!

Hop like a seal by springing off your hands and toes. How far can you hop?

Begin by marking a starting line on the floor. Then get into a push-up position behind the line. Only your toes and hands should be touching the floor. Keep your body straight and your arms bent at the elbows. If you want to make the event easier, keep your arms straight (as shown in the photograph), not bent at the elbows.

When you are ready, hop forward. Do this by springing up and forward with your arms and feet. Land in the push-up position after each hop, and then hop forward again. On each hop, your hands and feet must lift off the ground. Keep your body flat so that your hips do not rise higher than your head.

You must stop if you touch the floor with any part of your body other than your hands or toes.

In competition, the seal hoppers all start at the same time. The "seal" who hops the farthest wins.

At first, you probably will hop only a couple of times and travel a few feet, but keep practicing. The boys' record is 160 feet 2 1/8 inches. The girls' record is 136 feet.

Think About It

1. Where did the Eskimos get their idea for the seal hop?

2. Find out more about the Eskimos (Inuit). Write a short article telling what you learned.

Read a Book

Start the Unit Project

A Culture Fair Your class will plan a fair to celebrate the cultures in your community. As you read this unit, remember the ways people show their cultural heritage.

Use Technology

Visit The Learning Site at **www.harcourtschool.com** for additional activities, primary sources, and other resources to use in this unit.

1

Big Idea
Many kinds
of people
live in the
United States.

Vocabulary

unique

culture

Our Country of Many People

A mosaic is a picture made from many tiles of different colors. Our country is like a mosaic. It is made up of people of different ages and colors. They speak different languages and do different jobs. Many have **unique**, or special, talents.

Americans come from many cultures. A **culture** is the way a group of people live. It is what they eat, how they dress, and what they believe.

Americans also share something important. They believe that by respecting one another's ways they can live and work together in peace.

LESSON 1
Review

1 **Vocabulary** What **cultures** are in your community?

2 How can you learn about other cultures?

3 Interview someone with a unique job or talent.

Find Point of View

Vocabulary

point of view

▶ Why It Matters

Some people have a **point of view**, or way of looking at things, that is different from yours. What is important to people can tell us something about who they are or where they come from.

▶ What You Need to Know

Everyone has special interests. These interests give clues about the things the person thinks are important.

▶ Practice the Skill

Would a person using chopsticks eat rice or mashed potatoes?

Would a person using this bat play cricket or baseball?

Would a person playing bongo drums learn Latin music or opera?

Would a person who wears sandals live in a warm climate or a cold climate?

▶ Apply What You Learned

Bring something from home that represents your point of view and share it with the class.

People on the Move

Big Idea
Many people have moved to our country, bringing their cultures.

Vocabulary

explorer

pioneer

immigrant

People have always been curious about the world. Some of them became **explorers**. They traveled to find and learn more about new places. Long ago, explorers Christopher Columbus, Amerigo Vespucci, and Ferdinand Magellan sailed to North America. After that, people began moving to this continent, bringing their cultures with them.

GEOGRAPHY THEME

Who settled around Hudson Bay?

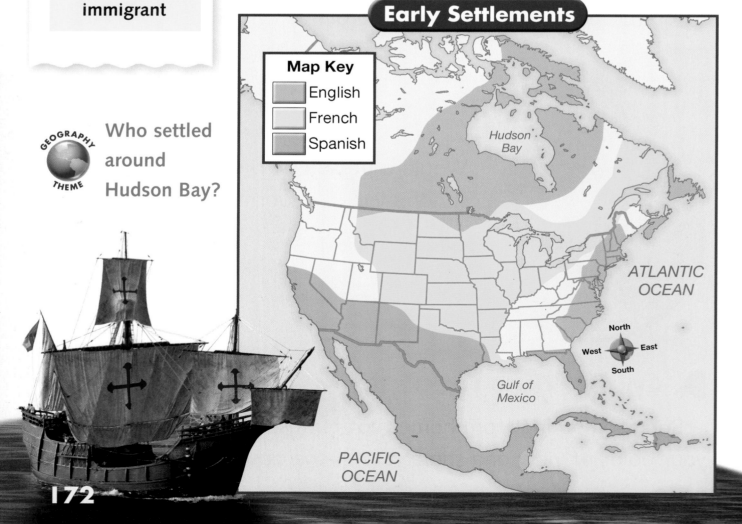

Early Settlements

Map Key
☐ English
☐ French
☐ Spanish

Hudson Bay

ATLANTIC OCEAN

North
West • East
South

Gulf of Mexico

PACIFIC OCEAN

At first most people settled along the coasts of America. Then pioneers began to move across the country. A **pioneer** is a person who first settles in a new place.

The pioneers traveled on foot, on horseback, and in wagons. Later, trains brought more people and goods until farms, ranches, towns, and cities spread across every part of the country.

Immigrants kept coming from other places around the world to live in the United States. They sailed here on big ships. Many of them landed at Ellis Island in New York Harbor. There they got permission to enter the United States.

Immigrants learned about their new home from their neighbors. In turn, the newcomers shared their cultures.

Immigrants are still finding new homes here. People also move from place to place in our country. New ideas and ways of living spread this way and become part of all our lives.

Sally Ride
born in 1951
Character Trait:
Heroic Deeds

Today some explorers are traveling to space. Sally Ride was the first American woman to fly into space. As a scientist, she spent a week on the space shuttle <u>Challenger</u> doing experiments. The work astronauts are doing today will help more people live and work in space someday.

MULTIMEDIA BIOGRAPHIES
Visit The Learning Site at
www.harcourtschool.com
to learn about other famous people.

GO
ONLINE

LESSON 2
Review

 Focus Skill

1 Generalize How do immigrants bring changes?

2 Vocabulary How do **explorers** and **pioneers** help a country grow?

3 Write a diary entry describing how you would feel about moving to a strange new place.

Follow Routes on a Map

Vocabulary

route

▶ Why It Matters

A map can show you not only where places are, but also how to get to them.

▶ What You Need to Know

The path you follow from one place to another is called a **route**. Highways are routes between towns and cities.

Practice the Skill

1 Which highway goes from Seattle to San Diego?

2 What direction would you travel on Highway 70 to go from St. Louis to Denver?

3 Which highway links many eastern cities?

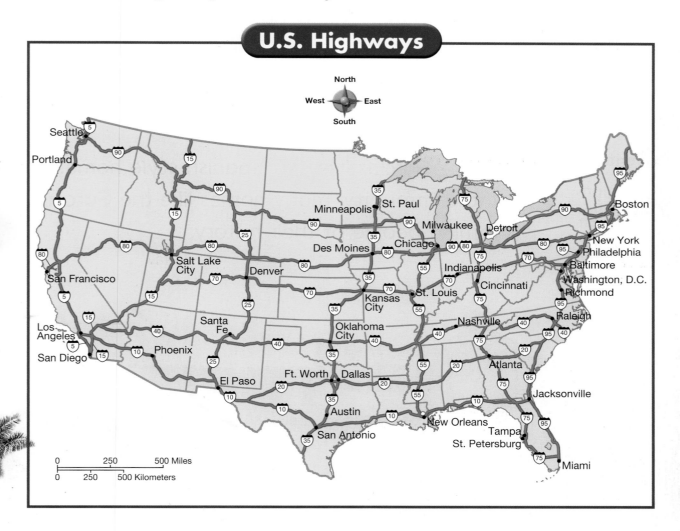

U.S. Highways

Practice your map and globe skills with the **GeoSkills CD-ROM**.

Apply What You Learned

Draw a map to show your route to school.

Big Idea
Families pass their culture from parent to child.

Family Heritage

María García lives in Arizona. Members of the García family have been living there for hundreds of years. They have a long heritage. **Heritage** is culture that is passed down from family to family over the years.

The Garcías live in a Spanish-style home. In the community, many homes like the Garcías' remind people of their history.

Land deed, 1673

María is learning to play the guitar. She especially likes some of the old Mexican songs she hears on the radio.

Mrs. García has a job at a community history center. She takes schoolchildren through the center. She explains the Spanish and Mexican heritage of Arizona.

Saul Volkoff's great-grandfather moved his family to New York in 1927. They came here because they wanted freedom to follow their **religion**, or belief in God. Saul's family is Jewish. Their religion is one of the oldest in the world.

Saul lives in a neighborhood with other families from Russia. His parents own a restaurant. They also send special foods around the country. The family works together and goes to temple together.

Aneesa Anwar lives in New Jersey across the river from Saul's family. The Anwars are newcomers from a country in Asia called Pakistan. They are learning English and making friends in their new country.

People often ask Aneesa about the clothes her parents wear. The Anwars are Muslims. They have many **traditions**, or special ways of doing things. Aneesa brought a prayer rug to school. It has belonged to her family for many years. She talked about some of her family's traditions.

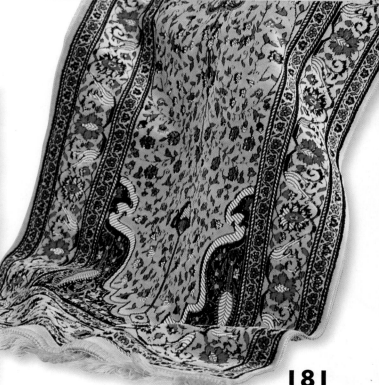

Kim Lee's grandmother helps his family remember their ancestors in Korea. An **ancestor** is a family member who lived long ago. She shows Kim photographs of their family.

There are many Koreans living in Seattle, Washington. Kim's dad designs Web pages for a computer company. Kim wants him to put their family's pictures on a Web page to share with other Koreans.

Family Reunion

As families grow, family members may move far apart. They can write letters and e-mails or phone their relatives. They can also plan family reunions. A reunion is a gathering of the family. Great-grandparents and grandparents, aunts, uncles, and cousins all join together for a fun celebration of their family's heritage.

LESSON 3
Review

1 **Vocabulary** What can you learn from a family's **heritage**?

2 Give an example of a family tradition.

3 Ask a parent or other adult to describe a family ancestor.

CHART AND GRAPH

Read a Bar Graph

▶ Why It Matters

Some information can be understood more easily if it is shown on a chart or graph.

▶ What You Need to Know

A **bar graph** is a drawing that uses bars to show the numbers of things. The title of the graph tells you what information it shows. Each bar stands for a different group being counted. Some bar graphs are read from left to right. Some bar graphs are read from bottom to top.

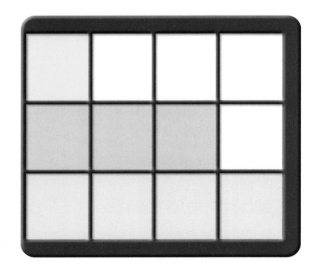
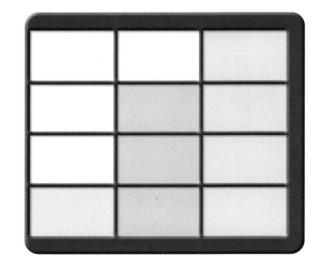

Family Ancestors

	0	1	2	3	4	5	6	7
Africa								
Asia								
North America								
South America								
Europe								
Australia								
Not sure								

▶ **Practice the Skill**

❶ How many children have ancestors from Europe?

❷ Are there fewer children with ancestors from Asia or from Africa?

❸ In which rows would you count someone whose ancestors were Native American?

❹ Why do you think the bar graph has a row labeled <u>Not sure</u>?

▶ **Apply What You Learned**

Work with classmates to make a bar graph. Show how many people you know from other continents.

Big Idea
Communities celebrate their cultures.

Vocabulary

holiday

custom

Community Celebrations

Americans celebrate many **holidays**, or special days, that began in other parts of the world. At these times people show everyone how proud they are of their cultures.

Chinese New Year

For Chinese people, the New Year is an important holiday. For two weeks, families follow many popular customs as they celebrate. A **custom** is the way a group of people does something. Chinese New Year has many customs. People give gifts, decorate homes and buildings, parade in costumes, and eat favorite Chinese foods. The Chinese also honor the elderly and remember their ancestors.

Mardi Gras

Mardi Gras means "fat Tuesday" in French. It is the day before Lent, the beginning of a season of the Roman Catholic Church. Lent is a serious time, so before it starts, everyone has fun on Mardi Gras. People like to dress up in costumes and march around the streets or go to parties.

Louisiana has the biggest Mardi Gras celebrations in the United States. The Cajun culture group there has a special custom. People go from door to door asking for food. They combine everything to make a big stew called gumbo for everyone to eat.

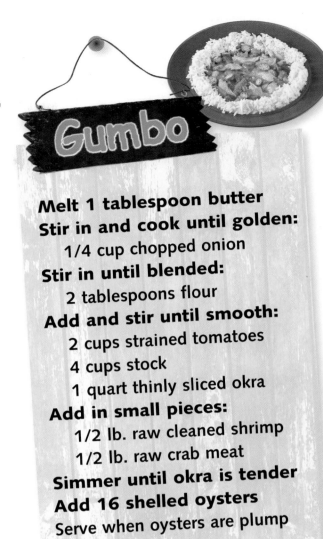

Gumbo

Melt 1 tablespoon butter
Stir in and cook until golden:
  1/4 cup chopped onion
Stir in until blended:
  2 tablespoons flour
Add and stir until smooth:
  2 cups strained tomatoes
  4 cups stock
  1 quart thinly sliced okra
Add in small pieces:
  1/2 lb. raw cleaned shrimp
  1/2 lb. raw crab meat
Simmer until okra is tender
Add 16 shelled oysters
Serve when oysters are plump

Cinco de Mayo

Cinco de Mayo is a fiesta, or holiday, celebrated by Mexican Americans. There are many street parties, at which people in beautiful costumes play music and dance with great energy. Parades of riders on horses remind everyone of the freedom Mexicans fought for many years ago.

piñata

Favorite Mexican foods are served. Some are very hot and spicy. Children play games and break open colorful piñatas stuffed with fruits, candies, and toys.

Kwanzaa

Kwanzaa is a week-long celebration in December. It began in 1966 as a way for African Americans to celebrate African traditions. On each of the seven days, families light a candle on the <u>kinara</u>. They remember their past and what is important to them.

kinara

Each day is special. One day is for thinking about being together. Another day is for music, dancing, and storytelling. On the last day, everyone joins in a <u>karamu</u>, or feast. Children often get books or handmade gifts as a reward for working hard during the year.

LESSON 4 Review

Focus Skill

❶ **Generalize** What can you learn about others through their holidays?

❷ **Vocabulary** Describe a **custom** from one of the holidays in this lesson.

❸ Make a greeting card for a special holiday in your community.

Expressions of Culture

Big Idea
People express their cultures through stories and the arts.

Vocabulary

language

Literature

People in every culture use **language** as a way to express themselves. People write stories and poems. The myths, legends, folktales, and fairy tales of a culture tell us what the people believe.

Moon Rope
Un lazo a la luna

AMERICAN TALL TALES
BY
Mary Pope Osborne
WOOD ENGRAVINGS BY
Michael McCurdy

Between Earth & Sky
LEGENDS OF NATIVE AMERICAN SACRED PLACES

Joseph Bruchac

THE GOLDEN BIRD

Retold from Grimm by Neil Philip

MISOSO
ONCE UPON A TIME
TALES FROM AFRICA
RETOLD BY VERNA AARDEMA
ILLUSTRATED BY REYNOLD RUFFINS

Some stories are told around the world.
They are the same story in different languages.

"Come!" he commanded. "You must try this rose-red slipper."

The servant girls gawked openmouthed as the Pharaoh kneeled before Rhodopis. He slipped the tiny shoe on her foot with ease. Then Rhodopis pulled its mate from the folds of her tunic.

"Behold!" cried Amasis. "In all this land there is none so fit to be queen!"

"But Rhodopis is a slave!" protested one of the servant girls.

Kipa sniffed. "She is not even Egyptian."

"She is the most Egyptian of all," the Pharaoh declared. "For her eyes are as green as the Nile, her hair as feathery as papyrus, and her skin the pink of a lotus flower."

The Pharaoh led Rhodopis to the royal barge, and with every step, her rose-red slippers winked and sparkled in the sun.

"Then she must deserve me as her husband," said the magistrate, "for this lucky shoe has led me to her."

"Another of Pigling's magic tricks!" hissed Omoni, pulling Peony to the palanquin. "My daughter will give you TWO shoes! That is twice as lucky!"

The magistrate looked at Omoni as if she had lost her wits; then he turned to Pear

Blossom and said, "I've luck enough if she who wears this one becomes my bride." Pear Blossom smiled, too shy to speak, and slipped the sandal on her foot.

Omoni stood staring, stiff as a clay statue, but Peony ran straight to the rice fields to find the magic ox. All she saw was a glimpse of its hooves as it galloped away.

THE EGYPTIAN CINDERELLA
by Shirley Climo • illustrated by Ruth Heller

THE KOREAN CINDERELLA
by Shirley Climo
Illustrated by Ruth Heller

Art and Architecture

You can visit museums in your community to find out about cultures. Paintings can tell about a group's history. Paintings, masks, and patterns woven in cloth can show you a group's traditions.

Mask from western Africa

Bark painting from Australia by Banapana

Kente cloth from Ghana

Buildings and gardens often remind us of the cultures in a community. Churches also show what groups of people live in a community.

English Victorian home

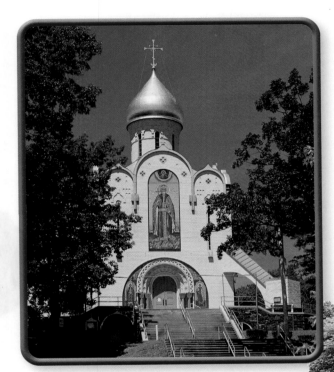

Russian Orthodox church

Spanish mission

Japanese garden

Music and Dance

Many communities celebrate their cultures with festivals. At these community gatherings you can enjoy the costumes, food, music, and dance from places around the world.

Scottish bagpiper

Irish folk dancers

Nigerian drummer

Dancers from Thailand

Look, listen, and learn.

1. **Vocabulary** How do people use **language** to express their culture?

2. What else can express culture?

3. Find out about something in your community that expresses culture.

Big Idea
Ideas spread
from place to
place.

Vocabulary

communication

Spreading Culture

You have read that people pass on their culture in their families. You know that holidays celebrate a culture's unique customs. You know, too, that people express their cultures in many ways.

You have read that culture is spread as people move to new places. Culture is also spread through different kinds of communication. **Communication** is the sharing of ideas.

Long ago, people shared ideas through stories told aloud. Most people could not read or write. Books were written by hand, so there were not many of them. Only a few people could afford a book.

quill pen

All this changed when Johannes Gutenberg invented a way to print more copies of books. Soon more people began to read and to write down their ideas.

Today books and newspapers are printed even more quickly and in greater numbers. We can also get information sent through satellites to our television sets.

Long ago, messages were carried by runners or by messengers on horseback. Over the years, inventions such as the telegraph and telephone made sending messages much easier and faster.

Telegraph, 1922

Telephone, 1922

Cellular phone, 1971

Fax, 1982

FAST FACT

In the past, carrier, or homing, pigeons delivered messages. They could fly up to 60 miles an hour for as far as 1,000 miles to find their way home again.

Today you can sit at a computer and find out about anything in the world through the World Wide Web. You can also send and receive messages called e-mail on the Internet.

LESSON 6
Review

① **Vocabulary** How has technology changed **communication**?

② Name three kinds of communication you use to learn about other cultures.

③ Send an e-mail to a school in another country. Ask questions about the culture there.

Read a Map of World Countries

▶ Why It Matters

When you read about other countries, it helps to see where they are on a map. It also helps to know what countries are their neighbors. Countries that are close together are more alike than different.

▶ What You Need to Know

There are more than 190 countries in the world. Russia is the largest country. China has the most people. The country of Australia fills the continent of Australia.

The World

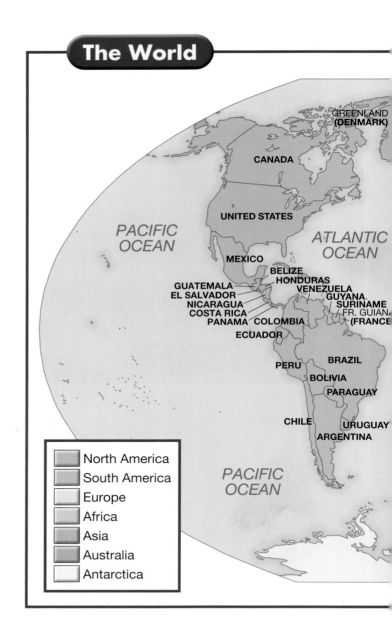

GREENLAND (DENMARK)

CANADA

UNITED STATES

PACIFIC OCEAN

ATLANTIC OCEAN

MEXICO

BELIZE
HONDURAS
GUATEMALA
EL SALVADOR
NICARAGUA
COSTA RICA
PANAMA COLOMBIA
ECUADOR

VENEZUELA
GUYANA
SURINAME
FR. GUIANA
(FRANCE)

PERU

BRAZIL

BOLIVIA

PARAGUAY

CHILE

URUGUAY
ARGENTINA

PACIFIC OCEAN

- North America
- South America
- Europe
- Africa
- Asia
- Australia
- Antarctica

MAP AND GLOBE SKILLS

Practice your map and globe skills with the **GeoSkills CD-ROM**.

200

Practice the Skill

1 Which continent has more countries, South America or Africa?

2 Which country is farthest north in Asia?

3 What countries are Ecuador's neighbors?

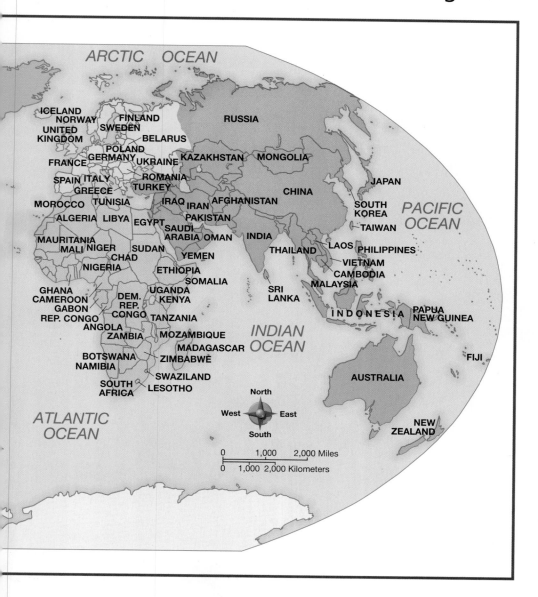

Apply What You Learned

When you read or hear about a country, find it on a map or globe. Keep a list of the countries.

VISIT A Crafts School

Traditions connect people with their heritage, or family history. Traditional crafts must be learned from people who know them. At a crafts school in North Carolina, students take classes to learn these skills.

Locate It
United States

North Carolina

What to See

An older student helps a child create a rug on a loom, a machine used for weaving.

A student dyes cloth by hand, using the deep blue color of the indigo plant.

Woodcarving

Yarn Dyeing

Bookmaking

A student paints designs on silk cloth.

Take a Field Trip

GO ONLINE

A VIRTUAL TOUR
Visit The Learning Site at **www.harcourtschool.com** to take virtual tours of other places of interest.

READING RAINBOW.

A VIDEO TOUR
Check your media center or classroom library for a video featuring a segment from Reading Rainbow.

203

Review and Test Preparation

Focus Skill Generalize

Use what you have learned about culture to complete the chart. Add one fact, and then write a general statement.

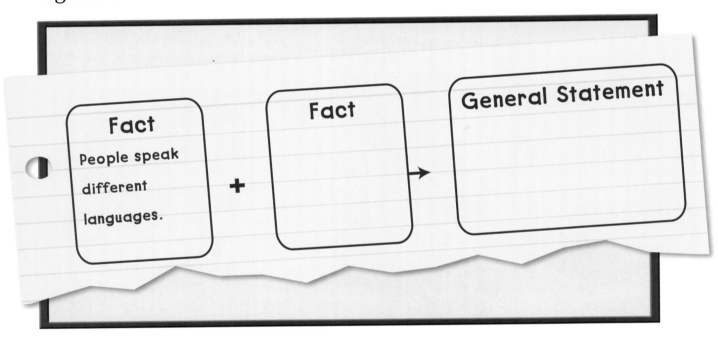

Fact

People speak different languages.

+

Fact

→

General Statement

THINK & WRITE

Draw a Custom Draw a picture of people following a custom from another country.

Tell a Story Write a short story about the people in the picture you drew.

Choose the word that matches the description.

1 Clara's great-great-grandmother was a pioneer. She raised her family on a farm.

2 During Kwanzaa, Chris lights the candles on the <u>kinara</u>.

3 Every year Gregory, like his father, puts on his kilt and marches in the Highland Parade.

4 We use our computer to learn about people in other countries.

> **heritage**
> (p. 178)
> **ancestor**
> (p. 182)
> **custom**
> (p. 186)
> **communication**
> (p. 196)

Recall Facts

5 How are Americans unique?

6 Where did many immigrants stop before entering the United States?

7 Describe a family tradition.

8 Which of these holidays begins a religious time?
   A Chinese New Year   **C** Mardi Gras
   B Cinco de Mayo   **D** Kwanzaa

9 Which of these is <u>not</u> part of a person's culture?
   F hair color   **H** art
   G language   **J** music

Think Critically

10 How does communication help spread ideas?

11 How does a culture's heritage add to a community?

Apply Chart and Graph Skills

The graph shows instruments from other countries. It tells how many children in a class want to learn to play each one.

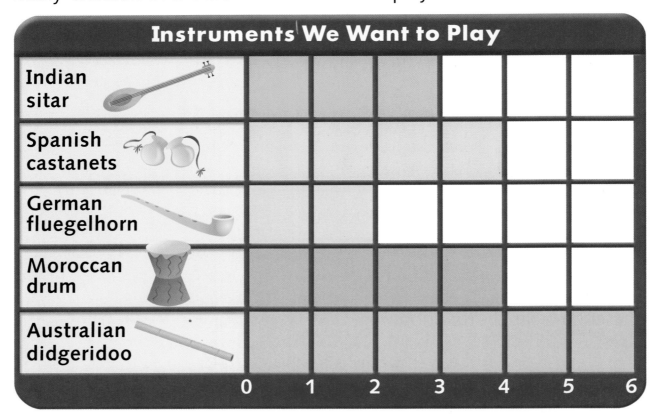

12 How many instruments are shown on the graph?

13 Which instrument did the most children choose?

14 How many children wanted to play the sitar?

15 Which instruments did the same number of children choose?

206

Florida Highways

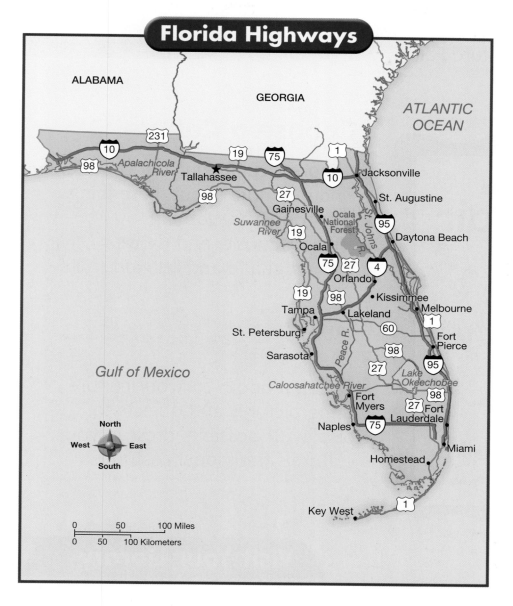

16 Which highway goes from Jacksonville to Tallahassee?

17 If you were traveling on Highway 75 from Tampa to Gainesville, what would you see along the way?

18 What highway takes you to Key West?

19 On which highway could you drive the entire east coast of Florida?

Unit Activities

Complete the Unit Project Work with a group to finish the unit project. Make a poster to advertise your Culture Fair.

GO ONLINE

Visit The Learning Site at **www.harcourtschool.com** for additional activities.

Culture Fair
Come, Look, Listen
Pine Elementary Gym
April 4 2:30 p.m.

Choose a Culture

Choose a culture in your community. Find out more about these things.
- its food and clothing
- its art, music, and dance
- its language and religion

Organize a Fair

Set up a booth for your culture. Bring pictures and objects to display. If possible, dress in your culture's traditional costume.

Visit Your Library

Chinatown by William Low. A boy and his grandmother enjoy the sights, smells, and sounds of New York City's Chinatown.

Chidi Only Likes Blue by Ifeoma Onyefulu. A rainbow of colors introduces the culture of people in a Nigerian village.

Different Just Like Me by Lori Mitchell. A young girl finds she has something in common with many different people.

Past and Present

A "winker" clock,
1865

Past and Present

" The present was an egg laid by the past that had the future inside its shell. **"**

—Zora Neale Hurston, <u>Moses, Man of the Mountain</u>, 1939

 Sequence

As you read this unit, do the following.

- List important events that happened in the past.
- Put the events in the order they happened.

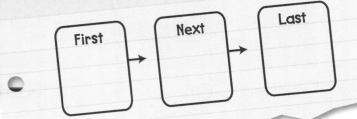

First → Next → Last

209

history   The study of what happened to people in the past. (page 222)

settler   One of the first people to make a home in a new place. (page 230)

landmark   A familiar object at a place. (page 239)

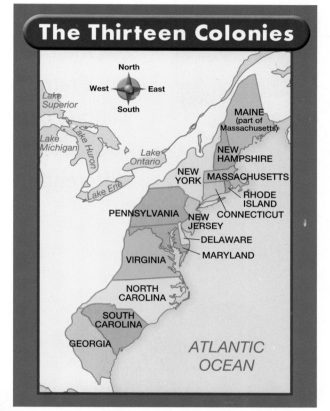

The Thirteen Colonies

North

West • East

South

Lake Superior

Lake Michigan

Lake Huron

Lake Ontario

Lake Erie

MAINE (part of Massachusetts)

NEW HAMPSHIRE

NEW YORK

MASSACHUSETTS

RHODE ISLAND

PENNSYLVANIA

CONNECTICUT

NEW JERSEY

DELAWARE

MARYLAND

VIRGINIA

NORTH CAROLINA

SOUTH CAROLINA

GEORGIA

ATLANTIC OCEAN

colony   A place that is ruled by another country. (page 238)

artifact   An object from another time or place. (page 224)

Growing Seasons

by Elsie Lee Splear
illustrated by Doug Bowles

One hundred years ago, the Lee family lived on a farm near the small town of Herscher, Illinois. They worked hard to grow their own food. Each **season**, or time of year, meant different jobs had to be done.

Planting Potatoes

The whole family helped Mama in her garden when early spring came and it was time to plant potatoes.

First Papa plowed and tilled the soil while my sisters and I helped Mama cut the seed potatoes into pieces. Each piece had to have a sprouting "eye." When the soil was soft, we went out into the garden with Mama and planted the potatoes in the furrows Papa had made. We used a measuring stick to make sure there was just the right distance between each piece of potato. It took the whole day just to plant the potatoes. Then Papa had to spread the soil over them again.

As the potato sprouts grew, Mama showed us how to hoe gently around each plant and how to pick the insects off the leaves. Finally, in the fall, the time came to lift the potatoes. Papa used the plow to bring them to the surface, and we girls picked up the potatoes one at a time, gently brushing off the loose dirt. We carried them by bushel baskets to a lumber wagon where the potatoes dried.

Finally, we stored them in wooden barrels in the cellar. There was always enough to last us through the winter. We loved all the different ways Mama cooked potatoes—fried, boiled, roasted, in soups, in casseroles. I could never decide which was my favorite.

Think About It

1. In what season are potatoes planted?

2. Draw a picture to show something you do during each season of the year.

Read a Book

Start the Unit Project

A Time Capsule Your class will make a time capsule to describe the time in which you live. As you read this unit, look for things that history tells about people of the past.

Use Technology

Visit The Learning Site at **www.harcourtschool.com** for additional activities, primary sources, and other resources to use in this unit.

Measuring Time

In the story <u>Growing Seasons</u>, the Lee family planted their fields in spring. They hoed and cared for the potatoes all summer. In fall, they harvested the crop and stored the food away for winter.

Long, long ago, in **ancient** times, people measured time by the growing seasons. They recorded the times for planting, caring for crops, and harvesting on a calendar. Today, in **modern** times, we use a calendar to record days, weeks, and months of a year.

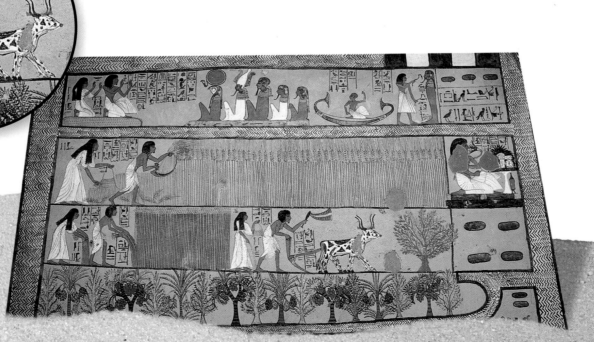

Ancient Egyptian wall painting

One of the first 365-day calendars was created in ancient Egypt. The story goes that Egyptian scientists were studying the skies. They saw that a very bright star would rise next to the sun every 365 days. That was about the time when the great Nile River began flooding its banks each year. The Egyptians made their calendar based on the star and the sun.

A CLOSER LOOK
Timepieces

Ancient people used many kinds of clocks. Some clocks needed the sun, water, or fire to measure time.

When do you think it might be hard to use a sundial to tell time?

sundial

candle clock

water clock

hourglass

early pendulum clock

digital quartz clock

Other people in ancient times created calendars. The Chinese used both the sun and the moon to measure time. The Mayas used a symbol for each of their eighteen months. The Mayan calendar was used and improved by later groups in Central America, such as the Aztecs.

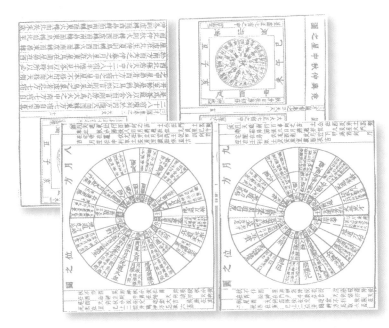

Chinese calendar

Mayan calendar

Pop **Uo** **Zip** **Zotz** **Tzec**

The calendar we use today was created by Aloysius Lilius, a doctor in Italy. People in Europe began using it in 1582, and in time it was used around the world.

People use calendars for more than measuring time. They use them to record the past, organize the present, and plan for the future.

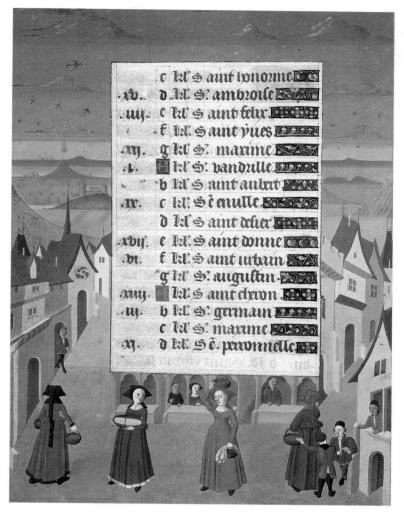

Early European calendar

LESSON 1
Review

Focus Skill

❶ **Sequence** What was the first tool people used to measure time?

❷ **Vocabulary** Why did people need calendars in **ancient** times?

❸ Make a chart that shows something in the past, present, and future.

CHART AND GRAPH

Read a Time Line

Vocabulary

time line

▶ Why It Matters

Another way to measure time is to use a time line. A **time line** tells you when and in what order things happened.

▶ What You Need to Know

You read a time line from left to right. The earliest events are on the left. This time line covers 50 years, with one mark for every 10 years.

1981 First shuttle is launched.

| 1960 | 1970 | 1980 |

1962 John Glenn first American to circle Earth.

1969 Neil Armstrong walks on moon.

1976 First spacecraft lands on Mars.

220

▶ Practice the Skill

In 1961 President John F. Kennedy said, "I believe that this nation should commit itself to achieving the goal, before this decade is out, of landing a man on the moon and returning him safely to Earth." Look at the time line below to see how well we did.

① When did Neil Armstrong walk on the moon?

② Did John Glenn make his second space flight before or after the landing on Mars?

③ When is the space station supposed to be finished?

▶ Apply What You Learned

Make a time line of events in your life.

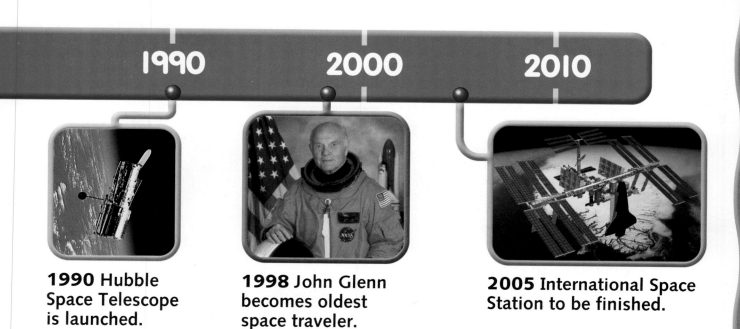

1990   2000   2010

1990 Hubble Space Telescope is launched.

1998 John Glenn becomes oldest space traveler.

2005 International Space Station to be finished.

Learning About the Past

History is made up of the stories people tell about the past. The past can be as long ago as ancient times or as near in time as yesterday. One way to learn about the past is through sources. A **source** is someone or something that can give information.

1 How are people sources?

grandparent

reenacter

librarian

2 How are places sources?

statues

FLORENCE MARTUS
1869 – 1943
SAVANNAH'S WAVING GIRL

historic markers

cemetery markers

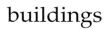

buildings

street signs

State Capitol in Carson City, Nevada

3 How are things, or **artifacts**, sources, too?

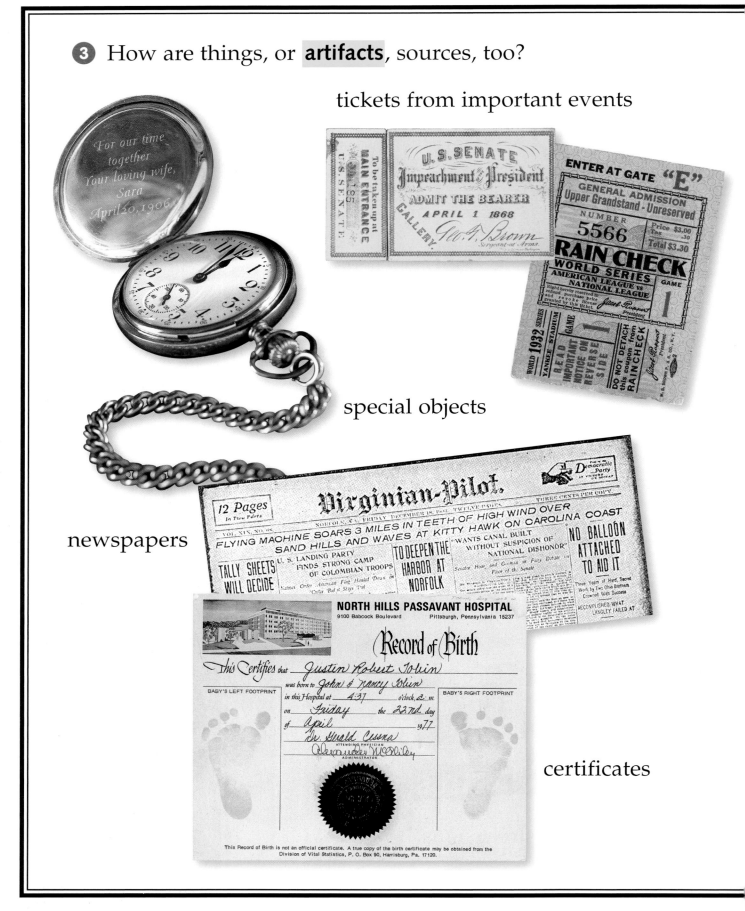

tickets from important events

special objects

newspapers

certificates

photographs

videos

Activity

Find out three interesting facts about your community's history. Get one from a person, one from a place, and one from a thing.

Research

Visit The Learning Site at
www.harcourtschool.com
to research other primary sources.

Predict a Likely Outcome

Vocabulary

predict

▶ Why It Matters

People can use what they learn from the past to **predict** the future, or tell what they think will happen.

▶ What You Need to Know

Here are some steps you can follow to predict a likely outcome.

Step 1 Think about what you already know.

Step 2 Find new information.

Step 3 Tell what you think will most likely happen next.

Step 4 Check whether what you predicted does happen.

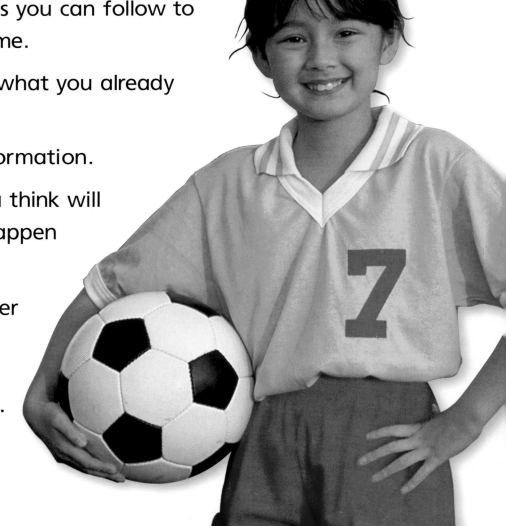

▶ Practice the Skill

1 Sandy's soccer team won six matches in a row. Predict whether Sandy's team will most likely win or lose its next match.

2 Sandy's soccer team is going to play a team whose players are two years older. What is the new information? Predict who will most likely win.

3 Check the glossary on page 334 to see if what you predicted is what happened.

▶ Apply What You Learned

Study the pictures below. What changes do you see? What information would you need to predict changes that will happen in the future?

past

present

Lesson

2

Big Idea
A community
has a history.

Vocabulary

museum

settler

Tracing a Community's History

Every community has a history. The stories people tell about it come from many sources. You can often find these sources in a local museum. A **museum** is a place where objects from other times can be seen. The Southwest Florida Museum of History in Fort Myers tells the story of the people and places of Southwest Florida.

THE FUTURE

MAXIMUM
SUSTAINABLE YI

The Calusa Indians were the first people to live in the Fort Myers area. They built villages by the Caloosahatchee River.

When Florida became part of the United States in 1821, settlers began moving to the Fort Myers area. A **settler** is someone who builds a home in a new place. Some of the settlers brought cattle and started ranches.

To protect the settlers, the army built a fort along the river. When a hurricane destroyed the fort in 1841, a new one was built farther inland. In 1850 the fort was made bigger and named Fort Myers.

After 1865, the fort was abandoned. The settlers took it apart and used the wood to build homes. By the 1870s, the community they started had homes, stores, and a school.

Locate It
United States

Fort Myers, Florida

Thomas Edison's estate

In 1885 a famous inventor named Thomas Edison visited Fort Myers. He fell in love with the village and the warm weather and decided to build a winter home there. He also built a laboratory he could work in and planted beautiful gardens.

• HERITAGE •

Caloosahatchee Manuscripts

This sculpture celebrates some of the early history of Fort Myers. One part lists the plants Thomas Edison used in his research. The other part tells about Florida's first Native Americans.

1885 was also the year the village of Fort Myers became a town. Only 349 people lived there, but that was enough to make it the second-largest town in southwest Florida. Cattle ranching was still an important business, and cattle sometimes walked through the downtown streets.

Drawing of cattle pens in downtown Fort Myers, 1880s

In 1905 the railroad came to Fort Myers. More people came to the town. Some people just visited, but others stayed. By 1911, the year Fort Myers became a city, more than 2,400 people lived there.

Atlantic Coast Line Railroad

First Street, 1909

When Thomas Edison first saw Fort Myers, he said, "There is only one Fort Myers, and 90 million people are going to find out." He was right. About 400,000 people live in the city today, and millions more visit every year. They come to enjoy the city's beauty and warm climate, just as Thomas Edison did many years ago.

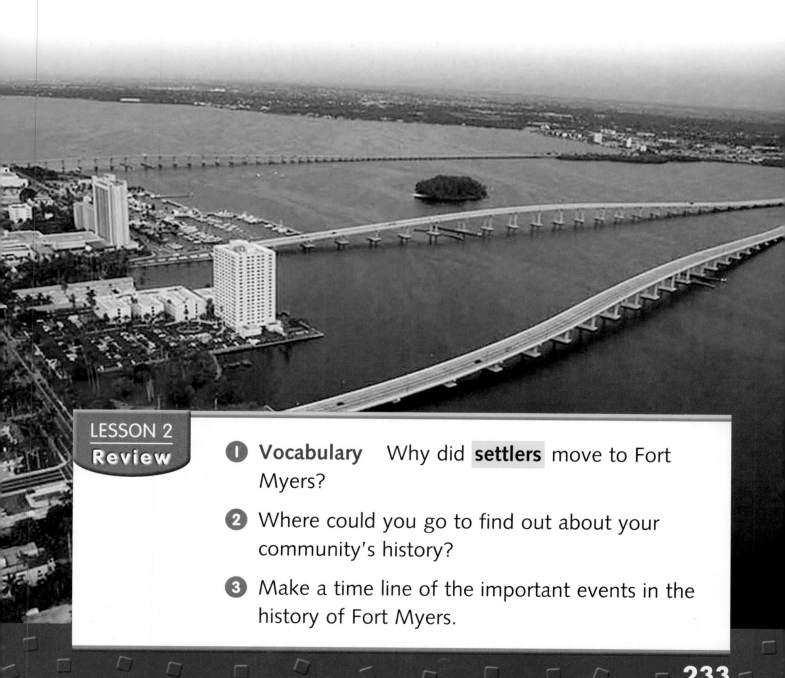

LESSON 2 Review

1. **Vocabulary** Why did **settlers** move to Fort Myers?

2. Where could you go to find out about your community's history?

3. Make a time line of the important events in the history of Fort Myers.

Identify Cause and Effect

Vocabulary

cause

effect

▶ Why It Matters

Changes happen for many reasons. It can be helpful to know why something happened.

▶ What You Need to Know

What makes something happen is a **cause**. What happens is an **effect**. You read that the building of the railroad caused more people to move to Fort Myers. The effect was a growing city.

Fort Myers

▶ Practice the Skill

There are other reasons that more people go to Fort Myers. Look at the following pictures. Explain how the building of an airport could affect the growth of Fort Myers.

1 Why do you think an airport was built in Fort Myers?

2 How can more visitors help Fort Myers grow?

▶ Apply What You Learned

Look for changes taking place in your community. Find out what has caused the changes.

3

Big Idea
Holidays help us remember our country's history.

Vocabulary
colony
independence
freedom
landmark

Celebrating Our Country's History

Some holidays celebrate the history of our country.

JAN	FEB	MAR	APR	MAY	JUN	JUL	AUG	SEP	OCT	NOV	DEC

Thanksgiving Day

Each year on Thanksgiving we remember the Pilgrims, the first English settlers in our country. The Wampanoag Indians showed them how to fish and grow food. Then they joined the Pilgrims in giving thanks for the first harvest.

As more people came to this country to settle, they met many groups of Native Americans. These groups were different from one another.

What foods did the Powhatan eat?

Independence Day

The first English settlers in North America built their colonies along the Atlantic Ocean. A **colony** is a place ruled by another country. England was very far away. The colonists were not always happy about following English laws.

On July 4, 1776, leaders in the colonies signed the Declaration of Independence. **Independence** is being free from rule by another country. The colonists said they were Americans and should have **freedom**, or the right to make their own choices. The English king did not agree.

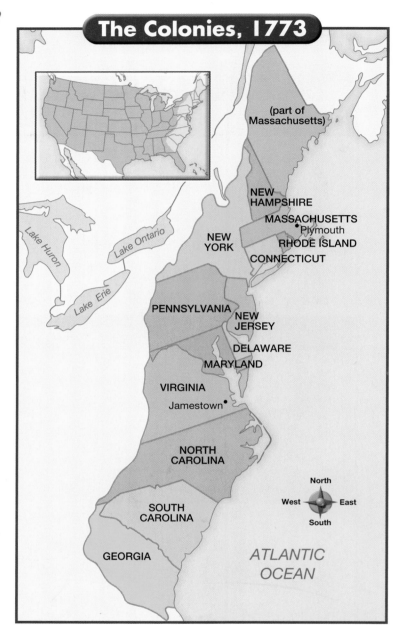

The Colonies, 1773

(part of Massachusetts)

NEW HAMPSHIRE

MASSACHUSETTS
Plymouth

NEW YORK

RHODE ISLAND

CONNECTICUT

Lake Huron

Lake Ontario

Lake Erie

PENNSYLVANIA

NEW JERSEY

DELAWARE

MARYLAND

VIRGINIA
Jamestown

NORTH CAROLINA

North
West — East
South

SOUTH CAROLINA

GEORGIA

ATLANTIC OCEAN

GEOGRAPHY THEME

In which colony is Plymouth?

238

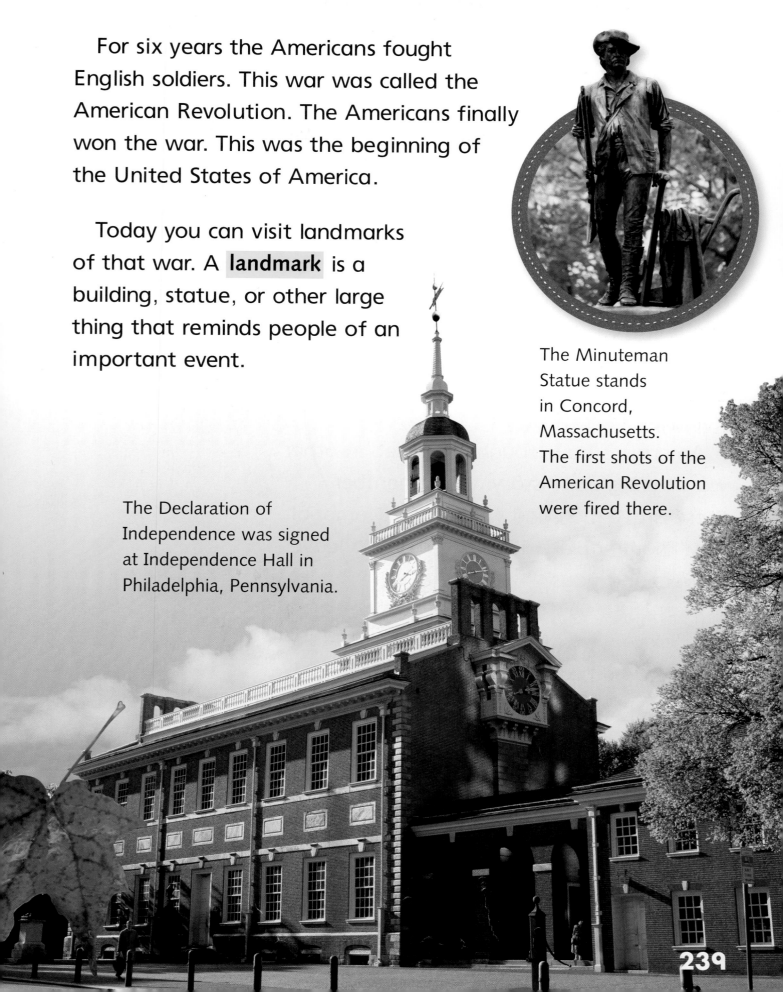

For six years the Americans fought English soldiers. This war was called the American Revolution. The Americans finally won the war. This was the beginning of the United States of America.

Today you can visit landmarks of that war. A **landmark** is a building, statue, or other large thing that reminds people of an important event.

The Minuteman Statue stands in Concord, Massachusetts. The first shots of the American Revolution were fired there.

The Declaration of Independence was signed at Independence Hall in Philadelphia, Pennsylvania.

Memorial Day

The first Memorial Day was held to honor people who died in the Civil War. The Civil War was fought between people in two parts of the United States. Some of the states of the South wanted to start their own country. The states of the North fought to keep the country together. The North won, but many Americans on both sides lost their lives.

Americans have fought and died in other wars during our history. We remember these brave men and women on Memorial Day, too. People visit cemeteries and leave flowers and flags.

Abraham Lincoln   1809–1865
Character Trait: Responsibility

President Lincoln was one of our most responsible leaders. He cared deeply for his country. His most difficult time was during the Civil War, in which Americans fought with each other. He stood on a battlefield and said, "These dead shall not have died in vain." Our country stayed strong because of his leadership.

MULTIMEDIA BIOGRAPHIES
Visit The Learning Site at
www.harcourtschool.com
to learn about other famous people.

Take pride in your country's past.

LESSON 3
Review

1 Vocabulary   What country started **colonies** along the Atlantic Coast?

2 Name two groups of Native Americans, and tell something about each.

3 Make a time line showing World War I, World War II, the Korean War, the Vietnam War, and the Gulf War.

Read a History Map

Vocabulary		
history map	region	settlement

▶ Why It Matters

A **history map** shows what places were like long ago. You can compare maps from different times to see how a place changes.

▶ What You Need to Know

Long ago, people moved to new **regions**, or parts, of our country. They built new homes to start **settlements**, or communities, across the West.

Practice the Skill

Study the history map to find the trails the settlers followed to move west.

1 Where does the California Trail begin?

2 Where does the Old Spanish Trail end?

3 Which two trails follow the Platte River?

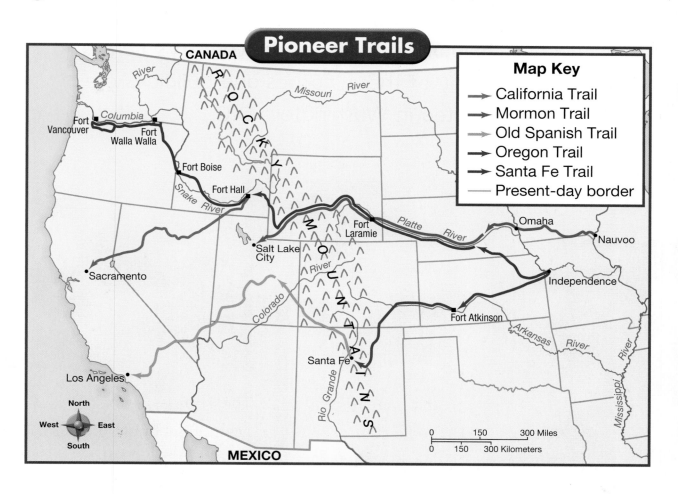

Pioneer Trails

Map Key
→ California Trail
→ Mormon Trail
→ Old Spanish Trail
→ Oregon Trail
→ Santa Fe Trail
— Present-day border

CANADA

River
Missouri River
Columbia
Fort Vancouver
Fort Walla Walla
Fort Boise
Snake River
Fort Hall
ROCKY
Salt Lake City
Fort Laramie
Platte River
Omaha
Nauvoo
Sacramento
River
MOUNTAINS
Colorado
Independence
Fort Atkinson
Arkansas River
Santa Fe
Rio Grande
Los Angeles
Mississippi River

North
West — East
South

MEXICO

0   150   300 Miles
0   150   300 Kilometers

Apply What You Learned

Compare the trail map to a highway map today to see how the country has grown.

Practice your map and globe skills with the **GeoSkills CD-ROM**.

Celebrating Heroes of the Past

Big Idea
Americans remember their heroes in many ways.

Americans have built **monuments** and **memorials** to honor the country's **heroes**. Many of these statues and buildings are located in Washington, D.C.

President Abraham Lincoln sits tall in the Lincoln Memorial. Lincoln guided the country through the Civil War and freed the slaves.

The Thomas Jefferson Memorial honors our third President, who helped write the Declaration of Independence.

The Washington Monument honors George Washington. He was a general in the American Revolution and our first President.

This is a memorial to President Franklin Delano Roosevelt and First Lady Eleanor Roosevelt. President Roosevelt led Americans during World War II. After the war Mrs. Roosevelt worked for peace around the world.

Monuments and memorials are found in many communities. People also honor heroes by naming schools, parks, and other places for them.

Thurgood Marshall

Thurgood Marshall wanted to be a lawyer. His mother, who was a teacher, encouraged him. However, the first law school Marshall tried to enter would not take African Americans.

Years later, as a lawyer, Marshall spoke to the Supreme Court about making all schools open to everyone. He won his case. In 1971 Thurgood Marshall was chosen to be the first African American Supreme Court justice. Now buildings around the country are named for him.

Louis Pasteur

A middle school in Orangevale, California, is named for Louis Pasteur. You can think about Pasteur every time you drink milk. He learned that some kinds of illness are caused by germs. He found a way to kill germs that get into milk and other foods.

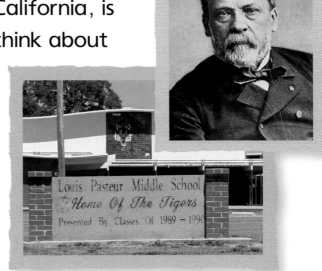

Golda Meir

At the University of Wisconsin, students study in the Golda Meir Library. Golda Meir was a Russian immigrant who grew up and taught school in Wisconsin. Later she moved to Israel. At the age of 71 she became the first woman to be the leader of Israel.

Golda Meir Library at the University of Wisconsin

247

Nobel Prize Winners

Each year people around the world who have done important work receive Nobel prizes. These prizes are given for work done in different kinds of science, in literature, and in keeping peace.

Marie Curie and Albert Einstein were scientists who won Nobel prizes. Marie Curie discovered a metal that could be used to cure illness. Albert Einstein used math to explain difficult ideas about time and space.

Nobel Prize

In 1964, Dr. Martin Luther King, Jr., won the Nobel Peace Prize. Dr. King was a minister. He worked to find peaceful ways for people of all colors to live together. His message was so important that Americans honor him with a holiday. The third Monday in January each year is Dr. Martin Luther King, Jr., Day.

248

Susan B. Anthony helped women get the right to vote.

Sacagawea guided explorers in the West.

Luis Muñoz Marín was the first governor of Puerto Rico.

Luis Muñoz Marín
USA 05
Governor, Puerto Rico

Sitting Bull was a famous Native American leader.

Sitting Bull
USA 28

Dennis Chavez was a senator from New Mexico.

Dennis Chavez
United States Senator
1888-1962
USA 35

Rachel Carson wrote about protecting the environment.

Rachel Carson
USA 17c

LESSON 4
Review

Focus Skill

1 Sequence What events led to Thurgood Marshall speaking to the Supreme Court?

2 Vocabulary Where in the United States can you find many **monuments** and **memorials**?

3 Make a poster showing what buildings in your community are named for people who have done important things.

Read a Map Grid

Vocabulary

map grid

▶ Why It Matters

One way to find places on a map is to use a map grid. A **map grid** is a set of lines that form columns and rows on a map. Knowing how to use a map grid makes it easy to find places on a map.

▶ What You Need to Know

Look at the grid on this page. Put your finger on the green square. Slide your finger to the left or right. You are on row C. Put your finger on the green square again. Slide your finger to the top or bottom. You are in column 4. To say where the green box is on the grid, you would say it is at C-4.

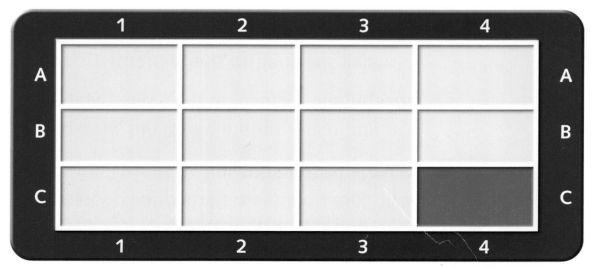

▶ Practice the Skill

1 Find the Petrified Forest. It is in square A-1. In which square is the Medora Visitor Center?

2 In which square are the Saddle Horse Rides?

3 Where is Prairie Dog Town?

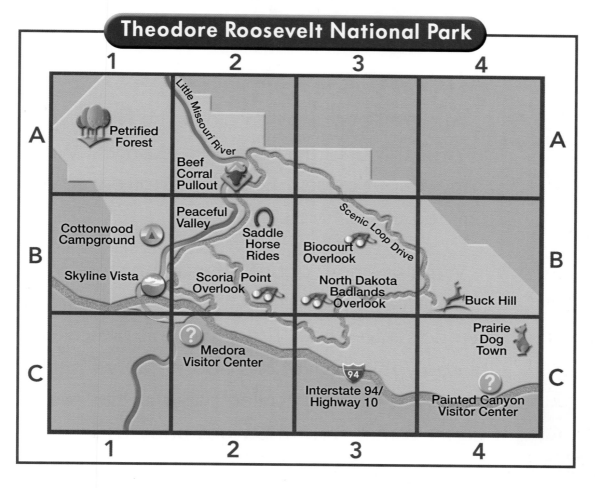

Theodore Roosevelt National Park

- Petrified Forest (A-1)
- Little Missouri River
- Beef Corral Pullout
- Cottonwood Campground
- Peaceful Valley
- Saddle Horse Rides
- Biocourt Overlook
- Scenic Loop Drive
- Skyline Vista
- Scoria Point Overlook
- North Dakota Badlands Overlook
- Buck Hill
- Medora Visitor Center
- Prairie Dog Town
- Interstate 94/ Highway 10
- Painted Canyon Visitor Center

▶ Apply What You Learned

Make a map of your neighborhood. Put a map grid on it. Tell a classmate the row and column of the square in which your home is located. See if he or she can find it.

Practice your map and globe skills with the **GeoSkills** CD-ROM.

Big Idea
People who lived long ago and far away have taught us many things.

Vocabulary
scribe
papyrus
maize

Contributions in World History

Ancient Egypt

Ancient Egypt started along the Nile River in Africa. Most Egyptians were farmers. We know about ancient Egyptian life from scenes painted on the walls of tombs.

We also know about Egyptian history from ancient writings. Writers called **scribes** carved symbols into stone. These symbols are called hieroglyphics. Egyptians also wrote with ink on a kind of paper called **papyrus**. Our word paper comes from the word papyrus.

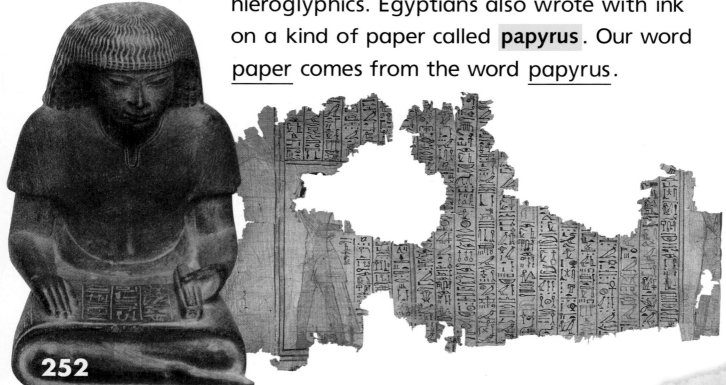

Ancient China

China is one of the oldest countries on Earth. More than 3,000 years ago, the Chinese had irrigation systems to water their crops. They built dams and highways. They had strong governments. They made beautiful works of art.

Some things we use today, such as fireworks and silk, came from ancient China. One of the most important things the Chinese gave us is paper. The Chinese made their paper from pieces of bark mixed with water. They pressed and dried the bark mush to make sheets of paper. The Chinese used carved blocks to stamp ink onto the paper. These were the first printed pages.

Ancient Americans

Thousands of years ago Native Americans lived in Central and South America. These ancient Americans built great cities.

A mural by Diego Rivera

The Aztecs lived in what is now Mexico. They built a huge city called Tenochtitlán on an island in the middle of Lake Texcoco. It had straight, wide streets. In the center was a giant pyramid used as a temple. In its marketplace sixty thousand people could gather to buy and sell goods. The Aztecs built this amazing city without all the machines we have for building today.

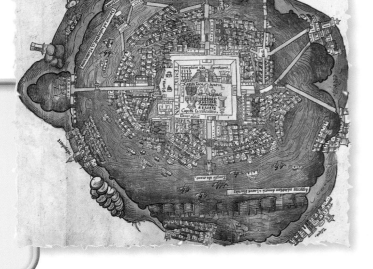

FAST FACT A legend tells how the Aztecs saw an eagle perched on a cactus at Lake Texcoco. This was a sign showing them where to build their great city.

Another large group of Native Americans, the Incas, lived in what is now Peru. They, too, built cities. They had a strong government that ruled large areas of land. The government made laws and provided services, such as food storage, to keep the Incas safe and healthy. Many of the foods that we eat today have come from the early Americans. Chilies, tomatoes, squash, and a kind of corn called **maize** are some of the foods they grew.

Inca Highways
Human Systems

The Incas lived in the high Andes Mountains of Peru. They built wide, paved roads to connect their cities. They had no horses, so mail was carried by runners. By passing it from one person to another, the runners could carry it 150 miles in a day.

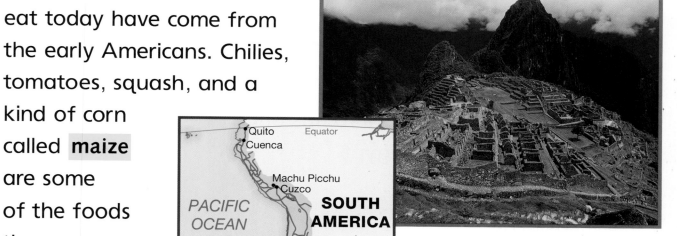

Quito   Equator
Cuenca

Machu Picchu
Cuzco

PACIFIC OCEAN   SOUTH AMERICA

LESSON 5
Review

❶ **Vocabulary** Why do you think **scribes** were important in ancient times?

❷ What groups of Native Americans built cities?

❸ Read a book about one of the ancient peoples in this lesson. Write a book report telling something you learned.

Read a Diagram

Vocabulary

diagram

▶ Why It Matters

You can find out how things work or how things are made by looking at a kind of picture called a **diagram**.

▶ What You Need to Know

The picture on the next page is a diagram of a pyramid. Pyramids were tombs built by the ancient people of Egypt.

▶ Practice the Skill

Study the diagram.

❶ Where were bodies mummified?

❷ What connected the Valley Temple to the pyramid?

❸ Where was the queen buried?

❹ What happened in the Mortuary Temple?

❶ The Valley Temple
Here the king's body was mummified.

5 The Tomb The king and his belongings were buried in a room inside the pyramid.

3 The Mortuary Temple Priests prayed to the king's spirit every day.

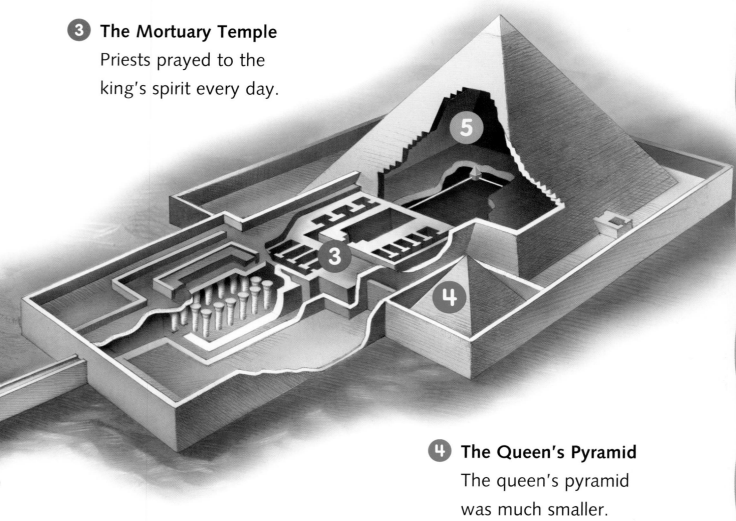

4 The Queen's Pyramid The queen's pyramid was much smaller.

2 The Causeway A walkway led to the pyramid.

▶ Apply What You Learned

Look for diagrams at home. Show or describe them to the class and explain how they are used.

VISIT Mount Rushmore

Get Ready

A memorial helps people remember a person or an event. Many memorials honor United States presidents. In South Dakota the Mount Rushmore National Memorial honors George Washington, Thomas Jefferson, Theodore Roosevelt, and Abraham Lincoln.

Locate It
United States

South Dakota

What to See

The Memorial honors Presidents from colonial to modern times whose work was important to United States history.

George Washington

Thomas Jefferson

Theodore Roosevelt

Abraham Lincoln

In 1927 artist Gutzon Borglum planned the memorial at Mount Rushmore. The sculpture took more than 14 years to complete.

Borglum made plaster models of the Presidents' faces. He used information from paintings, photographs, and written descriptions.

Workers used drills and dynamite to carve the solid rock of the cliff. The faces on Mount Rushmore are 60 feet high!

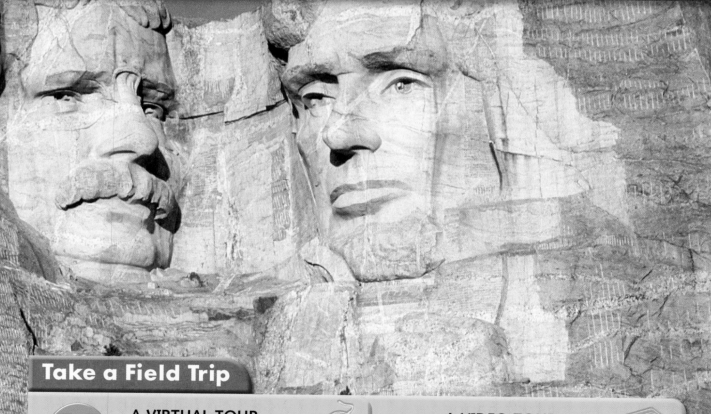

Take a Field Trip

GO ONLINE **A VIRTUAL TOUR** Visit The Learning Site at **www.harcourtschool.com** to take virtual tours of other monuments and memorials.

READING RAINBOW **A VIDEO TOUR** Check your media center or classroom library for a video featuring a segment from Reading Rainbow.

5 Review and Test Preparation

 **Sequence**

Put these events in the correct order.

Americans won their freedom in the American Revolution.
The Americans wrote the Declaration of Independence.
The English started colonies.

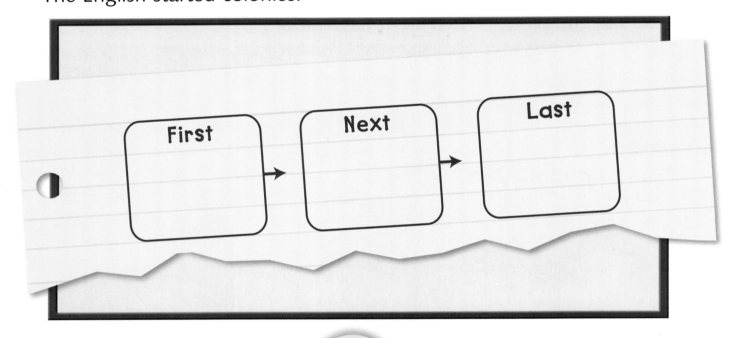

First → **Next** → **Last**

THINK & WRITE

Go Back in History Think of an event that happened in history. Use books and the Internet to find out about the event.

Report the News Write a news article telling about your event. Answer the questions who, what, when, and where.

Use Vocabulary

Change the underlined words to the correct vocabulary word.

1 A <u>person who built a home on the frontier</u> was a pioneer who helped our country grow.

2 The Gateway Arch, a <u>familiar sight</u> in St. Louis, reminds us of early pioneers.

3 Virginia was a <u>land ruled by another country</u>.

4 We studied an <u>object from the past</u> to learn more about ancient Egyptians.

5 <u>The study of the past</u> tells us who we are.

history
(p. 222)
artifact
(p. 224)
settler
(p. 230)
colony
(p. 238)
landmark
(p. 239)

Recall Facts

6 What tools do we use to measure time?

7 Who were the first people to live in Fort Myers?

8 Tell something you learned about a hero in this unit.

9 On which holiday do we remember the American Revolution?

   A Thanksgiving   **C** Memorial Day

   B Labor Day   **D** Independence Day

10 Who was President during the Civil War?

   F George Washington   **H** Thomas Jefferson

   G Abraham Lincoln   **J** Franklin Roosevelt

11 What are some ways to learn about the past?

12 How are ancient people a part of our history?

Apply Chart and Graph Skills

The International Space Station

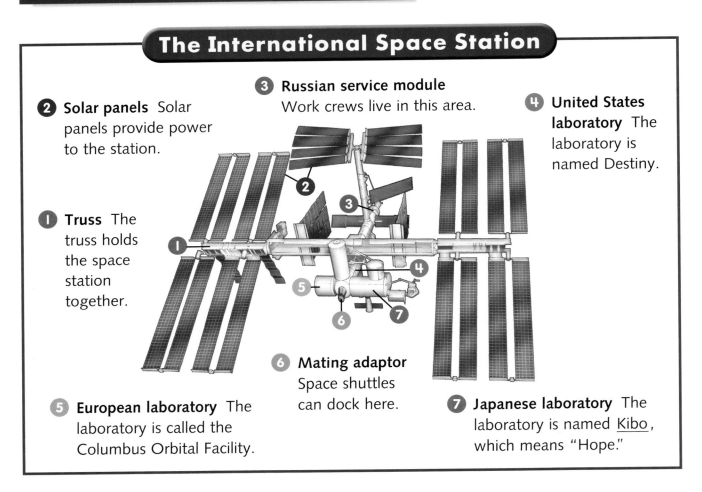

2 Solar panels Solar panels provide power to the station.

3 Russian service module Work crews live in this area.

4 United States laboratory The laboratory is named Destiny.

1 Truss The truss holds the space station together.

5 European laboratory The laboratory is called the Columbus Orbital Facility.

6 Mating adaptor Space shuttles can dock here.

7 Japanese laboratory The laboratory is named Kibo, which means "Hope."

13 What is the source of power for the space station?

14 What holds the space station together?

15 Where will experiments be done?

16 What is the name of the U.S. laboratory?

Apply Map and Globe Skills

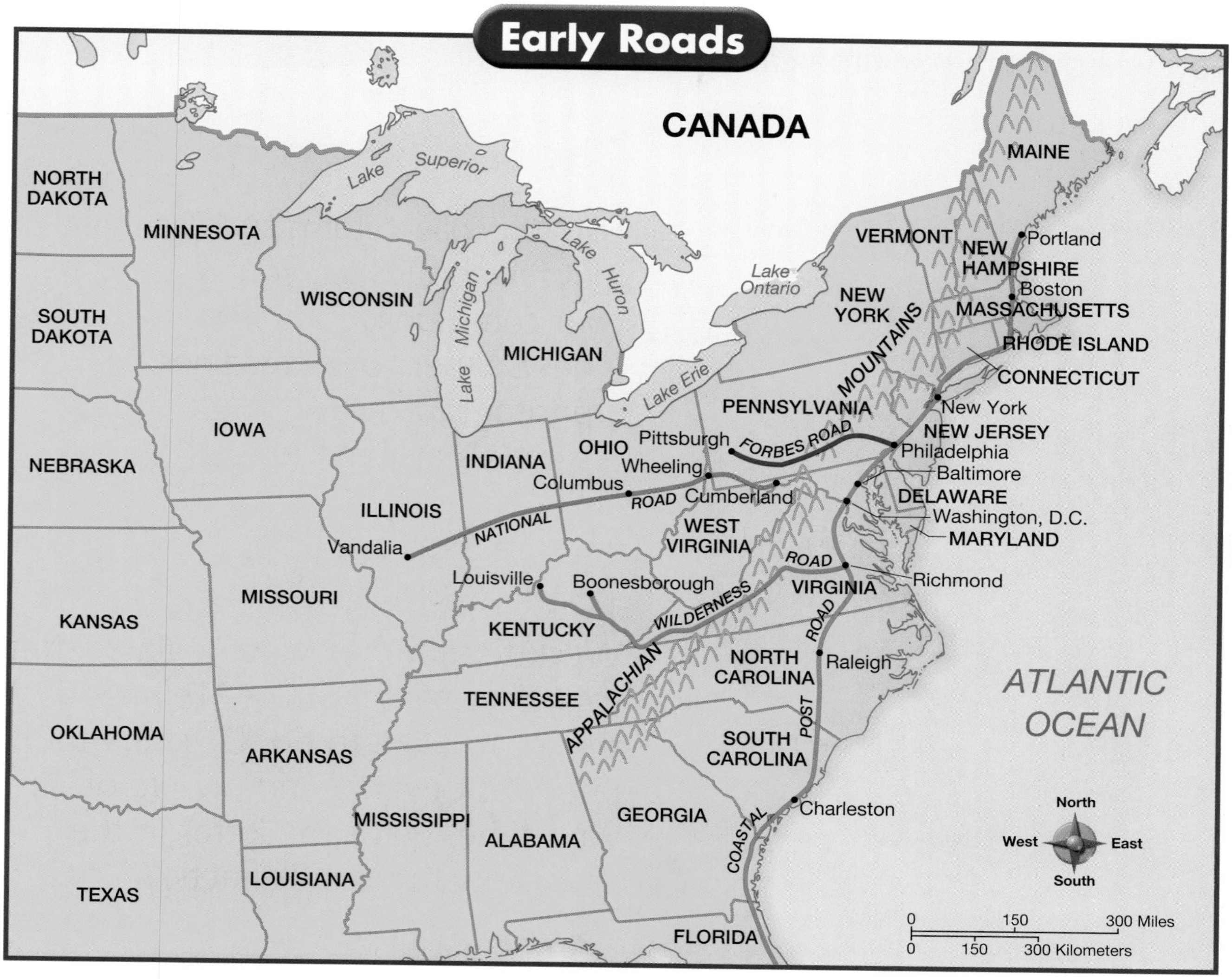

17. Name two cities on the Coastal Post Road.

18. Which road crossed the Appalachian Mountains into Kentucky?

19. What road went from Cumberland to Vandalia?

20. Which road connected Pittsburgh to the Coastal Post Road?

Unit Activities

GO ONLINE

Visit The Learning Site at www.harcourtschool.com for additional activities.

Complete the Unit Project Work with your class to finish the unit project. Decide what you will put in your time capsule and where you will store it.

Choose Artifacts

List and collect items such as these that tell about you, your school, and your community.

- newspapers or magazines
- photographs
- symbols and models

Write a Letter

Work together to write a class letter to a class of the future. Tell about things you like to do. Describe the important events and people of your time. Place the letter in the capsule with your artifacts.

Visit Your Library

Right Here on This Spot by Sharon Hart Addy. Objects dug from the ground give clues to the past.

Kindle Me a Riddle by Roberta Karim. A pioneer father shares riddles with his daughter to explain the past.

The Tomb of the Boy King: A True Story in Verse by John Frank. Explore the mysteries of Egypt's King Tutankhamen.

264

People at Work

A manual typewriter, early 1900s

6

People at Work

" Whatever your life's work is, do it well. **"**

— Dr. Martin Luther King, Jr., in a speech at Montgomery, Alabama, 1956

(Focus Skill) Summarize

As you read this unit, do the following.

- List main ideas about the work people do and the way they spend their money.
- Summarize what you learned.

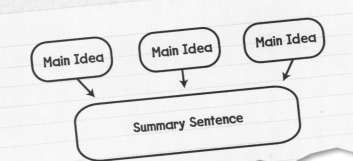

Main Idea → Main Idea → Main Idea →

Summary Sentence

producer   A person who makes, grows, or sells goods. (page 277)

income   The money people earn for the work they do. (page 286)

free enterprise   The freedom to start and run any kind of business. (page 286)

consumer   A person who buys and uses goods and services. (page 279)

factory   A building in which people use machines to make goods. (page 282)

transportation   Ways of carrying people and goods from one place to another. (page 300)

WORK

by Gary Paulsen
illustrated by Ruth Wright Paulsen

It is keening noise and jolting sights,
and hammers flashing in the light,
and houses up and trees in sun,
and trucks on one more nighttime run.

SONG

It is fresh new food
to fill the plates,
and flat, clean sidewalks
to try to skate,
and towering buildings
that were not there,
hanging suddenly
in the air.

It is offices filled with glowing screens
and workers making steel beams,
and ice-cream cones to lick and wear,
and all the pins that hold your hair.

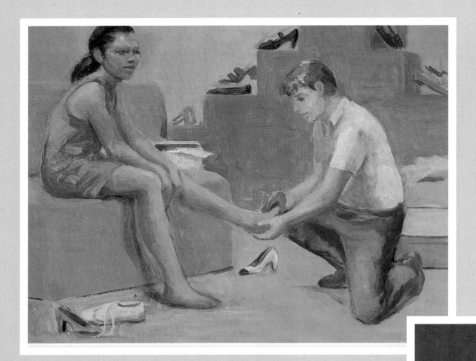

It's gentle arms that lift and hold,
and all the soldiers brave and bold,
and help to fit the brand-new shoes,
and hands to show you books to use.

It is people here and people there,
making things for all to share;
all the things there are to be,
and nearly all there is to see.

And when the day is paid and done,
and all the errands have been run,
it's mother, father in a chair,
with tired eyes and loosened hair.
Resting short but loving long,
resting for the next day's song.

Think About It

1 How do farmers and truck drivers depend on one another?

2 Write a job description for a job that interests you.

Read a Book

Start the Unit Project

Career Day Your class will plan a Career Day to find out about different jobs. As you read this unit, think about the kind of work people do and what interests you.

Use Technology

GO ONLINE

Visit The Learning Site at **www.harcourtschool.com** for additional activities, primary sources, and other resources to use in this unit.

1

Goods and Services

Big Idea
Everyone depends on people who provide goods and services.

Vocabulary

goods

services

In "Worksong" you met many people with different kinds of jobs. You depend on people like these every day. Some workers, such as the grocer, the shoe seller, and the steelmaker, provide goods. **Goods** are things that can be bought and sold.

Think about the things you use every day. Some workers grow or make these goods and others sell them.

Stores are places where people can buy all kinds of goods. What goods can you buy in your community?

In "Worksong" you also met many people who provide services. A **service** is work done by others for pay. The construction worker, the truck driver, and the nurse provide services. What services can you buy in your community?

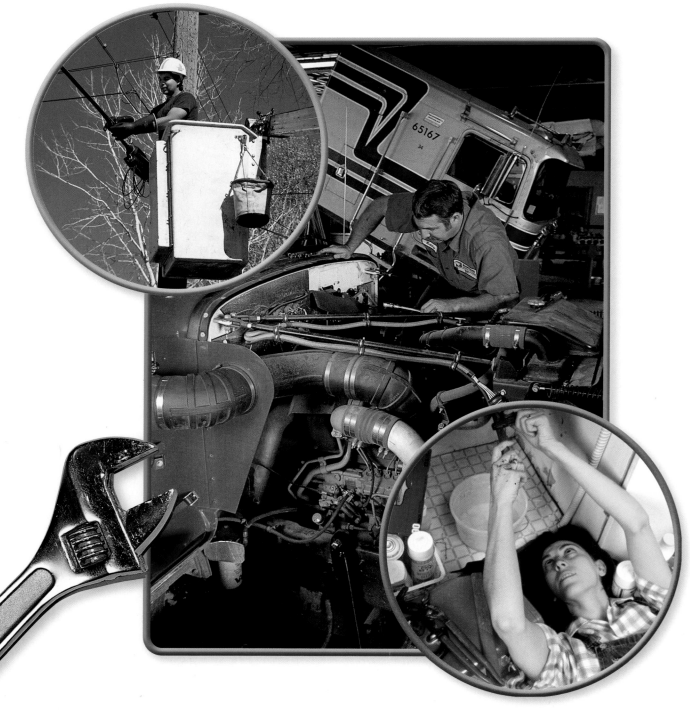

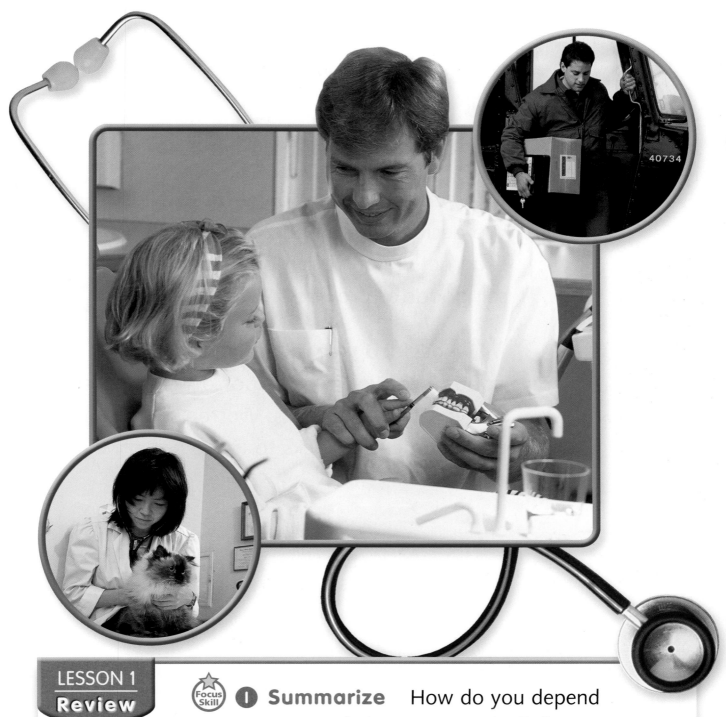

Focus Skill

1 Summarize How do you depend on people in your community?

2 Vocabulary What is the difference between **goods** and **services**?

3 Interview your neighbors about their work. Make a table showing which ones provide goods and which ones provide services.

Producers and Consumers

Big Idea
Businesses need both producers and consumers.

Vocabulary
business
producer
consumer

My class needed money for a field trip. We decided to start a business. A **business** is an activity in which people make or sell goods or provide services.

We decided we would make and sell goods. We liked the idea of office supplies. Everyone offered ideas. Warren suggested we paint interesting rocks to make paperweights.

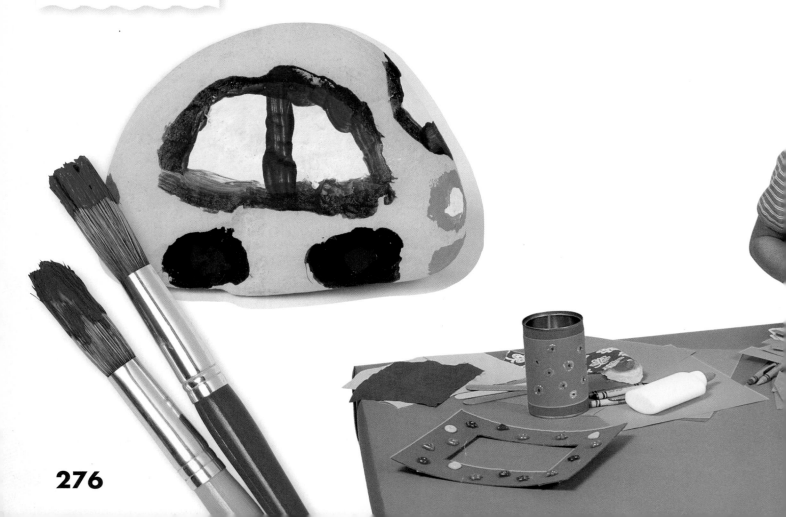

Judy knew how to decorate wooden clothespins to hold papers. Linsey showed us how to glue pretty scraps of paper to cardboard to make bookmarks.

Everyone in the class became a producer. **Producers** make the goods or provide the services people buy in a community.

After we produced the goods, we were ready to sell them. We set out the office supplies and decided on prices. Then we invited our families and friends to come and shop.

Warren's mother was the first to buy. She bought a paperweight. She was a consumer. A **consumer** buys goods or services. We are all consumers.

My classmate Lisa had made a picture frame. I thought it might look good with a picture of my cat Goldie in it. So I bought the picture frame. Now you can call me a producer *and* a consumer!

LESSON 2
Review

❶ **Vocabulary**   How are **producers** different from **consumers**?

❷ Explain how you can be both a producer and a consumer.

❸ Write a paragraph telling what you think makes a business successful.

A Visit to a Factory

Big Idea
Many kinds
of resources
are used to
produce goods.

Vocabulary
raw material
factory
manufacture

Ray and Dan Noble own a tomato canning company in Hobbs, Indiana. The Noble family has been canning tomatoes for more than 75 years. Cans of their whole tomatoes, stewed tomatoes, diced tomatoes, and tomato juice go to schools, markets, and restaurants.

RAY BROS. & NOBLE
CANNING

Ray Packing Company, September, 1925

Locate It
United States

Hobbs,
Indiana

Raw Materials

Ray and Dan need **raw materials** to produce their goods. They need tomatoes. They grow some themselves and buy more from nearby farmers. When they buy tomatoes, they are consumers as well as producers.

FAST FACT

The idea of serving tomato juice began at the French Lick Springs Hotel in Indiana in 1917. The chef often cooked a tomato dish. He and a waiter thought it would be a good way to use the juice from the tomatoes.

Noble Farms
TOMATO JUICE
46 FL. OZ. (1 QT. 14 OZ.) 1.36 L

Workers

In a **factory**, or building where people use machines to make goods, each worker has a special job. Ray and Dan run the business. Office workers keep track of the orders and workers' pay. Other workers watch over the machines that clean, move, can, and cook the tomatoes. Still others pack the cans of tomatoes and load the boxes onto trucks.

Machines

It takes all kinds of machines to make, or **manufacture** , canned tomatoes and tomato juice. Machines called conveyors move the tomatoes from place to place. Other machines wash and peel the tomatoes. After tomatoes are canned and cooked, large machines stack the cans. The canned goods are sent around the country. Someone in Lakeland, Florida, could be eating Indiana tomatoes.

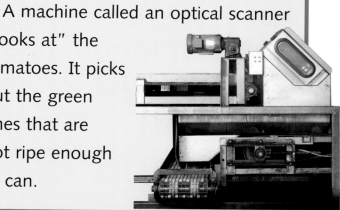

SCIENCE AND TECHNOLOGY

Optical Scanner

A machine called an optical scanner "looks at" the tomatoes. It picks out the green ones that are not ripe enough to can.

LESSON 3
Review

Focus Skill ❶ **Summarize** How are tomatoes used to make goods?

❷ **Vocabulary** What is a **factory** ?

❸ Invite someone from a factory to visit your class. Make a list of the resources the factory uses.

Follow a Flow Chart

Vocabulary

flow chart

product

▶ Why It Matters

A **flow chart** shows the steps needed to make or do something. You can use a flow chart to show the steps workers follow to produce a product. A **product** is something that is made by nature or by people.

▶ What You Need to Know

The title of the flow chart tells what it is about. Each picture has a sentence that describes the step. Arrows show you the order of the steps.

▶ Practice the Skill

1 What does the flow chart show you?

2 What is the first step?

3 What happens after the tomatoes are put into cans?

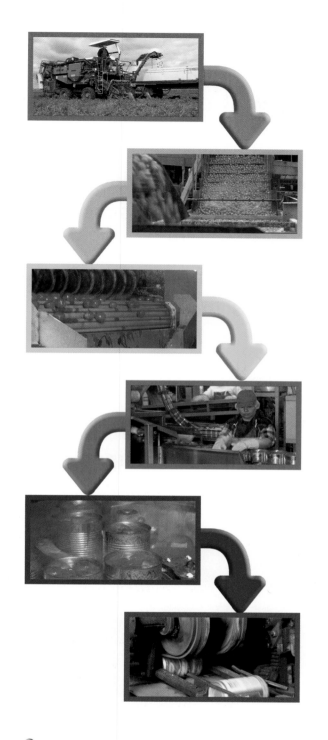

1 The tomatoes are harvested.

2 A conveyor takes the tomatoes to be washed.

3 A machine peels the tomatoes.

4 The tomatoes are put into cans.

5 The tomatoes are cooked in cans.

6 The cans are sealed and put into boxes.

▶ Apply What You Learned

Think about a job you know how to do. For example, list the steps for setting the table or making your bed. Use your list to make a flow chart. Share it with a family member.

CHART AND GRAPH SKILLS

Work and Income

Vocabulary

income

free
enterprise

bank

interest

People make or sell goods or provide services to earn money. Hector earns money by watering plants for his neighbors. He also shovels snow in the winter. The money he earns for his services is his **income**.

Hector saves some of the money he earns. He shares some, too, and spends the rest. The freedom to decide how to make money and what to do with it is called **free enterprise**.

Saving

Hector saves some of his money in a bank until he wants to spend it. A **bank** is a business that keeps money safe. Money in a bank earns more money. This extra money is called **interest**.

Hector's grandmother gave him money on his birthday. Since he wants to save money for college, he puts that money in the bank.

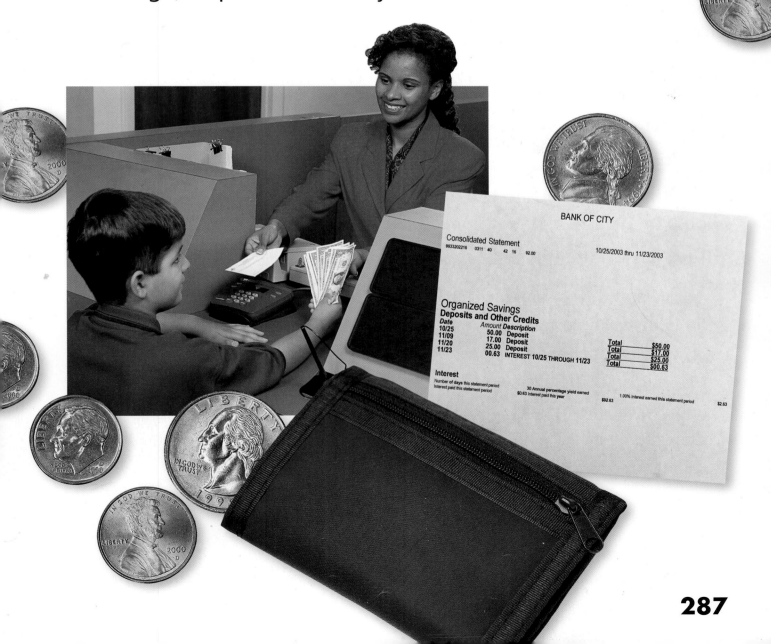

BANK OF CITY

Consolidated Statement
9933202216   0311   40   42   16   92.00   10/25/2003 thru 11/23/2003

Organized Savings
Deposits and Other Credits

Date	Amount Description		
10/25	50.00 Deposit		
11/09	17.00 Deposit	Total	$50.00
11/20	25.00 Deposit	Total	$17.00
11/23	00.63 INTEREST 10/25 THROUGH 11/23	Total	$25.00
		Total	$00.63

Interest
Number of days this statement period
Interest paid this statement period   30 Annual percentage yield earned
                                              $0.63 interest paid this year $92.63   1.00% interest earned this statement period $2.63

Sharing

Hector shares some of his money. He gives it to his church. His church uses the money for repairs and for special programs for children. Hector's church shares some of its money with another church in the Dominican Republic.

• BIOGRAPHY •

William (Bill) H. Gates
born in 1955

Character Trait: Kindness

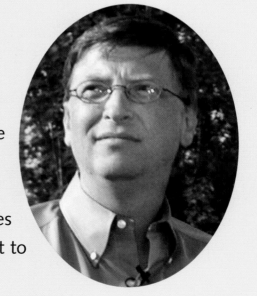

Bill Gates thinks computers are useful tools for people. He started a company to help make computers easier and better for people to use. His company has done so well that he is now one of the richest people in the world. Bill Gates shares some of the money he earns by giving it to libraries and schools that need computers.

MULTIMEDIA BIOGRAPHIES
Visit The Learning Site at **www.harcourtschool.com** to learn about other famous people.

GO ONLINE

Spending

Hector also spends some of the money he earns. He enjoys that!

Where You Live and Work

When you are older, you will need to get a job to earn an income. The kind of job you decide on will affect where you live and where you work.

LESSON 4 Review

1. **Vocabulary** How do people earn an **income**?

2. What might people do with the money they earn?

3. Find out about someone who has shared money to help people in your community.

Skills

CITIZENSHIP

Make Choices When Buying

▶ Why It Matters

When you go shopping, you see many things you want to buy. You need to make a choice about how to spend your money wisely.

▶ What You Need to Know

When there is not enough of something, we say that it is **scarce**. Money can be scarce. Resources can also be scarce, causing goods to be more expensive. You have only a certain amount of money to spend, so you cannot buy everything. You must decide what you are willing to give up to get what you want.

290

▶ Practice the Skill

Imagine that you have five dollars to spend. You want to buy a book. You also want to rent a movie. You do not have enough money to do both.

1 If you decide to buy the book, what do you give up?

2 If you decide to rent the movie, what do you give up?

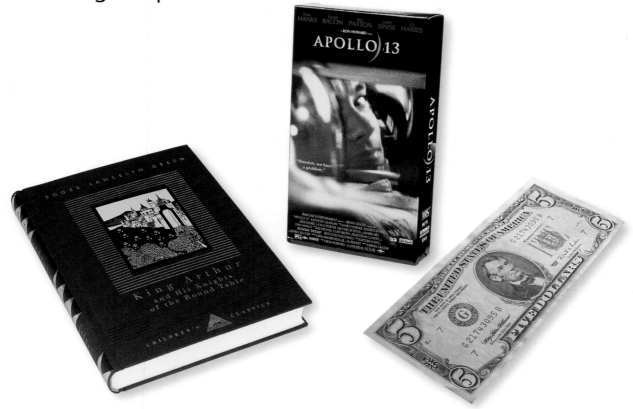

▶ Apply What You Learned

Think about your choices the next time you go shopping. Write down how you spend your money. Then explain your choices to a family member.

History of Money

Long ago people used to **barter**, or trade, for things they needed. They might trade eggs for cloth. Some people used stones, shells, feathers, or salt to buy things. Today people pay for goods and services with coins, paper money, checks, and credit cards.

1 Why do you think people started to use kinds of money?

Ancient money

First coins, Turkey

First paper money, China

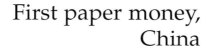

2 Why do you think money changes over time?

Early American money

Massachusetts Pine Tree shilling, 1652

Continental U.S. bill, 1776

U.S. silver dollar, 1794

Greenback dollar bill, 1862

③ What do other countries call their money?

Chinese yuan

Indian rupee

Zimbabwean dollar

Japanese yen

Mexican peso

Euro

Canadian dollar

4 How can checks and credit cards be used to pay for things today?

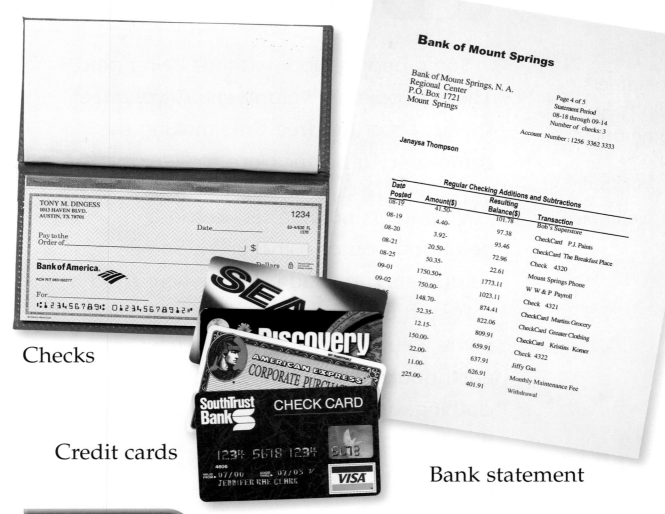

Checks

Credit cards

Bank statement

Activity

Draw a diagram of a dollar bill. Write what the symbols on it mean.

Research

Visit The Learning Site at
www.harcourtschool.com
to research other primary sources.

Big Idea
Volunteers help their community.

Vocabulary

volunteer

People Make a Difference

Some people work without being paid. These people are volunteers. A **volunteer** spends his or her free time making the community a better place to live.

Volunteers provide services in a neighborhood or community. Some volunteers run food banks, where food is collected and given to people who need it. Some volunteers help people after an earthquake or flood. They collect food, clothing, and blankets for people who need them.

Jimmy Carter   born in 1924
Rosalynn Carter   born in 1927
Character Trait: Respect

Jimmy Carter was once President of the United States. His wife, Rosalynn, was First Lady. After they left the White House, the Carters served as volunteers on a project called Habitat for Humanity. A habitat is a place to live, and humanity is people. These volunteers build or repair homes for people who need this help.

MULTIMEDIA BIOGRAPHIES
Visit The Learning Site at
www.harcourtschool.com
to learn about other famous people.

GO ONLINE

Do a good deed.

LESSON 5
Review

1. **Vocabulary**   How can **volunteers** help a community?

2. What can you do to help volunteers?

3. Make a list of volunteer groups in your community.

Goods from Near and Far

No country can grow or make all the goods its people need and want. Countries get goods from one another by making a trade. **Trade** is the exchange of one thing for another.

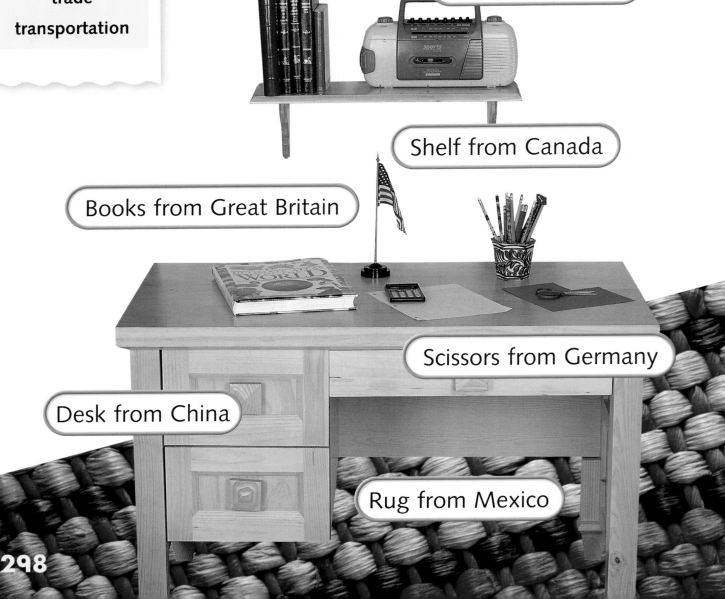

Radio from Japan

Shelf from Canada

Books from Great Britain

Scissors from Germany

Desk from China

Rug from Mexico

Trading Partners

Country	Products		
Canada	lumber	maple syrup	newsprint
Mexico	fruit/vegetables	pottery	rugs
Japan	cameras	computers/games	CD players
Germany	clocks	tools	toys
Great Britain	books	clothing	silverware
China	furniture	silk cloth	tea

What product made in Germany might you buy?

Countries use many kinds of **transportation** to move goods from one place to another. Goods travel between countries by train, truck, ship, and plane.

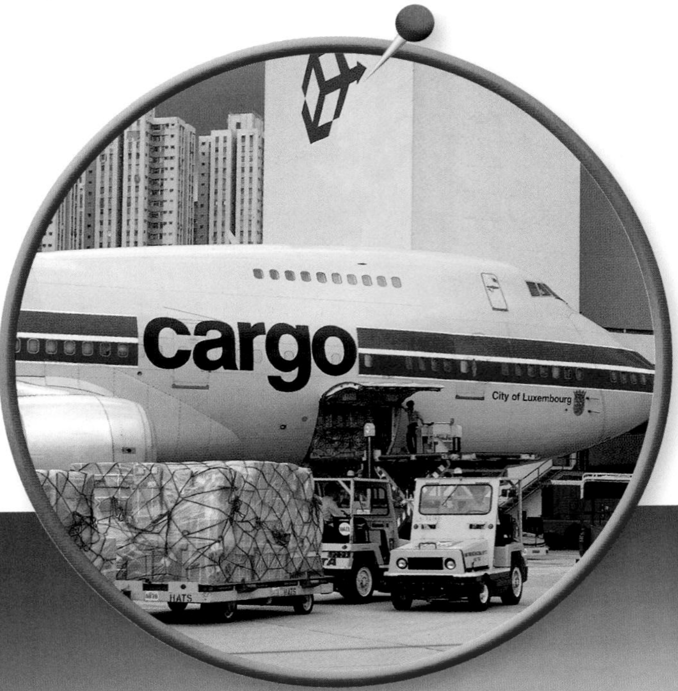
cargo
City of Luxembourg

How are goods moved from the United States to Canada and Mexico?

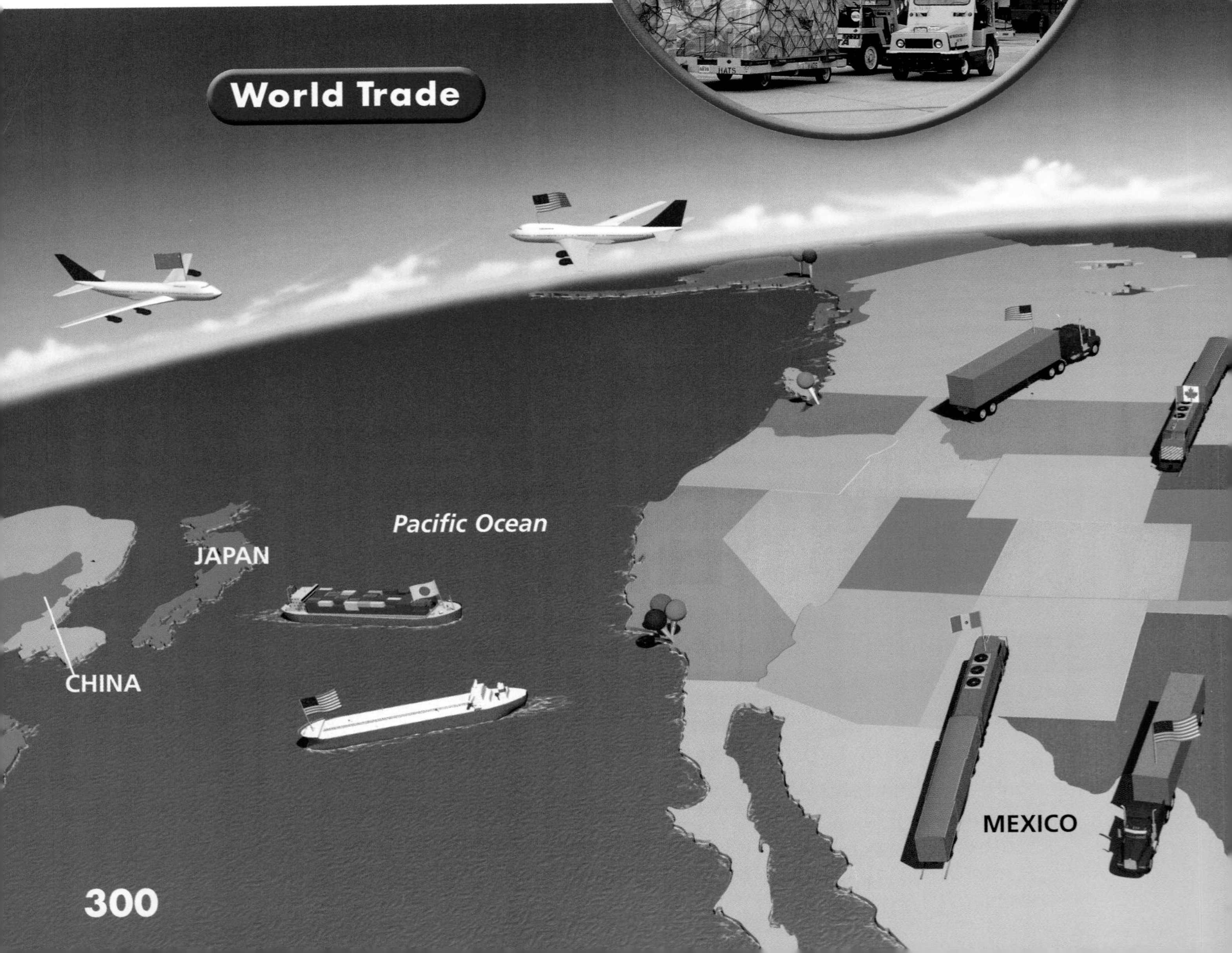
World Trade
Pacific Ocean
JAPAN
CHINA
MEXICO

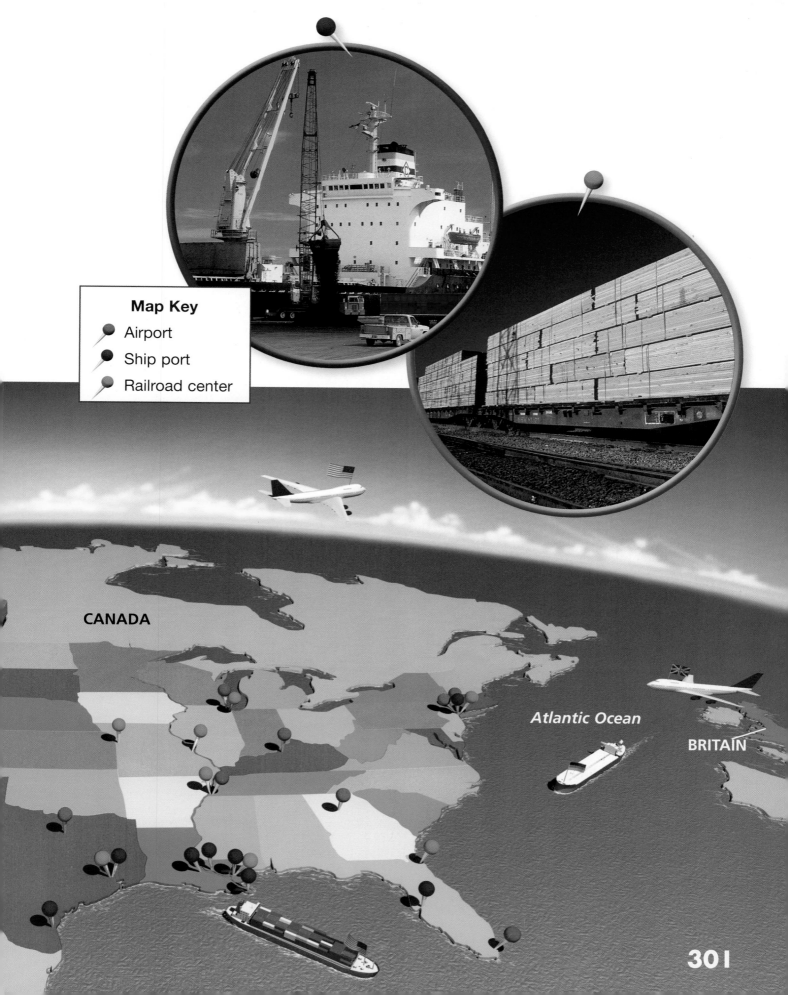

Map Key
- 🔴 Airport
- 🔴 Ship port
- 🔴 Railroad center

CANADA

Atlantic Ocean

BRITAIN

Trains

In 1869 the world's first coast-to-coast railroad was finished. Trains could then carry people and goods from one side of the United States to the other.

Trucks

Huge trucks carry tons of goods across our country. Refrigerated trucks can carry food and other goods that need to be kept cold.

Ships

Many people think that Robert Fulton invented the steamboat. He really just made it better. His steamboat made moving people and goods by river easier and faster.

Planes

In 1932 Amelia Earhart was the first woman to fly across the Atlantic Ocean alone. At that time, pilots flew small propeller planes. Those planes could not fly as high, far, or fast as today's jet planes. When Amelia Earhart tried to fly around the world, her plane ran out of fuel over the Pacific Ocean. It was never found.

Because of Earhart and other early pilots, people became more interested in flying. Today planes connect people around the world.

LESSON 6 Review

❶ **Vocabulary** How does **trade** help people meet their needs?

❷ What goods from other countries can you find in your community?

❸ Make a map to show how goods get to your community from around the world.

MAP AND GLOBE

Read a Product Map

Vocabulary

product map

▶ Why It Matters

Some maps can tell you about the products and resources of a place. You can use the map to understand more about the kinds of jobs people do there.

▶ What You Need to Know

A **product map** uses symbols to help you identify products and resources. Australia has many valuable resources.

▶ Practice the Skill

1 What products are shown in the map key?

2 What resource could you find near Kalgoorlie?

3 In what part of Australia would you find most of the cattle?

4 Near what cities can you find fruit growing?

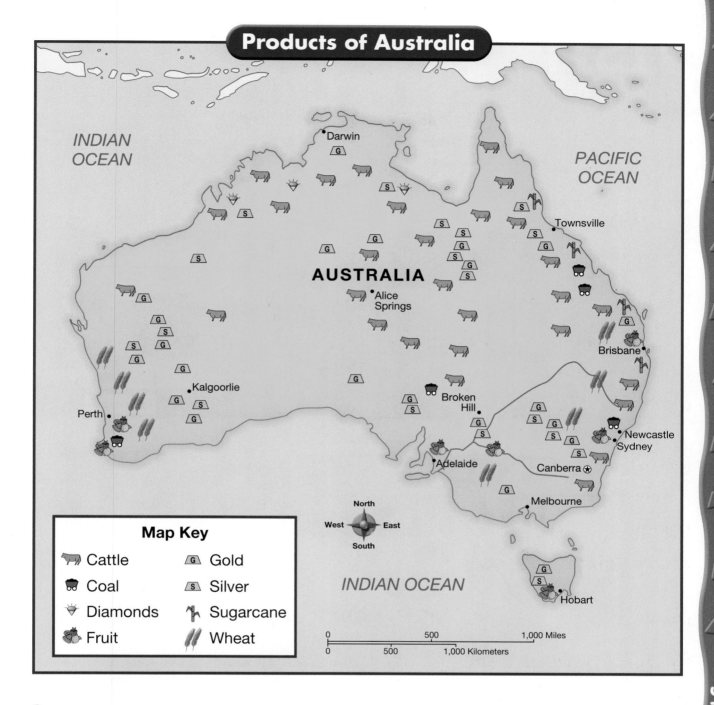

Products of Australia

Map Key

Symbol	Product	Symbol	Product
Cattle		Gold	
Coal		Silver	
Diamonds		Sugarcane	
Fruit		Wheat	

▶ Apply What You Learned

Find out what products are in your state. Draw symbols on a map of your state to show where some of these products and resources are located.

Practice your map and globe skills with the **GeoSkills CD-ROM**.

A CRAYON FACTORY

Get Ready

At a factory in Pennsylvania, workers and machines have been making crayons since 1903. Today the factory runs 24 hours a day, mixing melted wax and color to create more than a hundred different crayon colors. Over 10 million crayons are made every day.

Locate It
United States

Pennsylvania

What to See

1 Workers pour the hot, colored wax into molds that shape the crayons.

2 Crayons are carefully removed from the molds and checked.

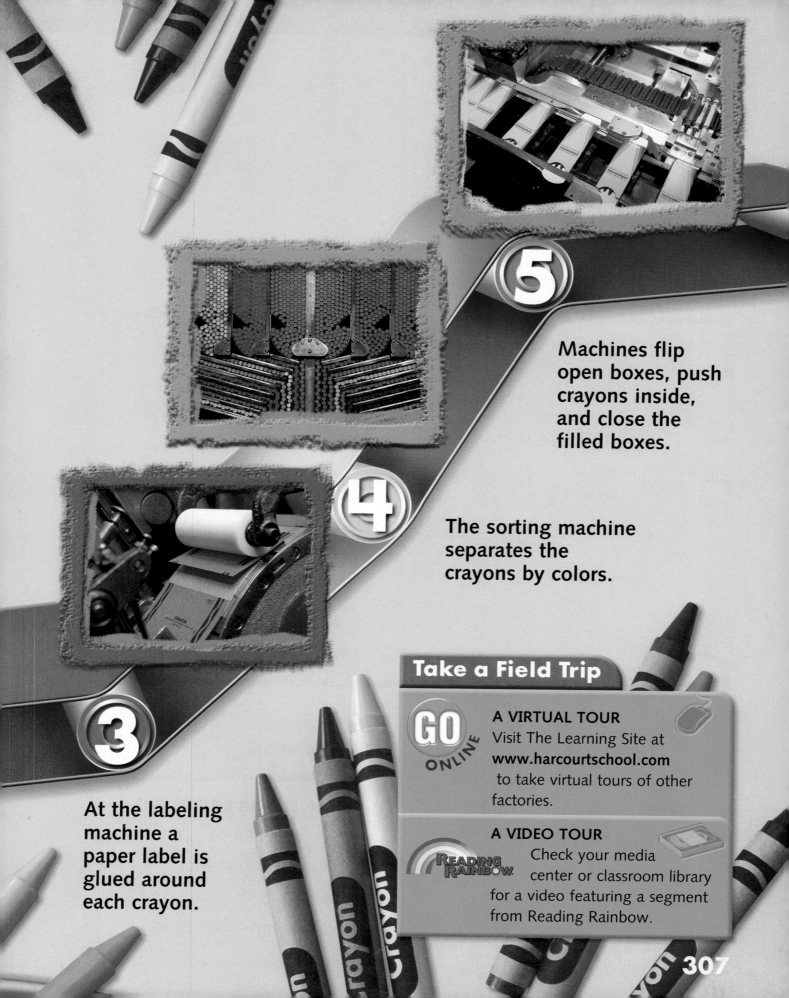

5 Machines flip open boxes, push crayons inside, and close the filled boxes.

The sorting machine separates the crayons by colors.

4

3 At the labeling machine a paper label is glued around each crayon.

Take a Field Trip

GO ONLINE

A VIRTUAL TOUR
Visit The Learning Site at **www.harcourtschool.com** to take virtual tours of other factories.

A VIDEO TOUR
READING RAINBOW. Check your media center or classroom library for a video featuring a segment from Reading Rainbow.

Review and Test Preparation

Focus Skill — Summarize

Write what you have learned in this unit about summarizing.

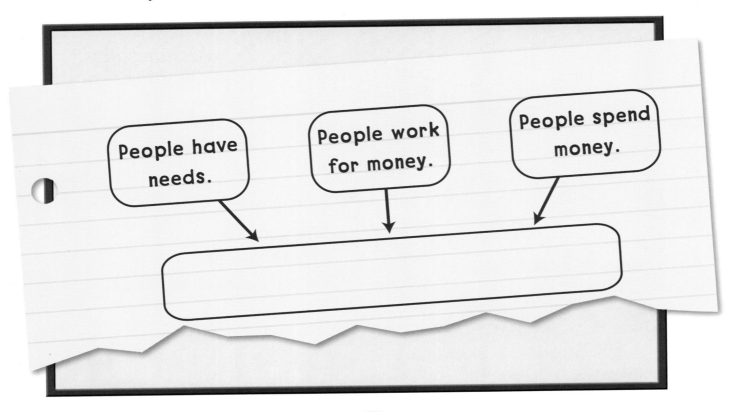

People have needs.

People work for money.

People spend money.

THINK & WRITE

Invent a Product Think of a new product. Ask yourself why people might need or want to have your product.

Write an Advertisement Write an advertisement about your product. Use words that will make people want to buy it.

Use Vocabulary

Match each word with its definition.

1 The freedom to start and run any kind of business

2 A person who makes, grows, or sells goods

3 Ways of carrying people and goods from place to place

4 A person who buys and uses goods and services

5 The money people earn for the work they do

6 A building in which people use machines to make goods

producer
(p. 277)

consumer
(p. 279)

factory
(p. 282)

income
(p. 286)

free enterprise
(p. 286)

transportation
(p. 300)

Recall Facts

7 How can a person be both a producer and a consumer?

8 What three things do factories need to make goods?

9 Why do people work?

10 Which of these workers sells a service?

A farmer

B baker

C potter

D plumber

11 Which kind of transportation is <u>not</u> used to move goods?

F bus

G plane

H train

J boat

12 How can scarcity affect what you buy?

13 Why is trade with other countries important?

Apply Chart and Graph Skills

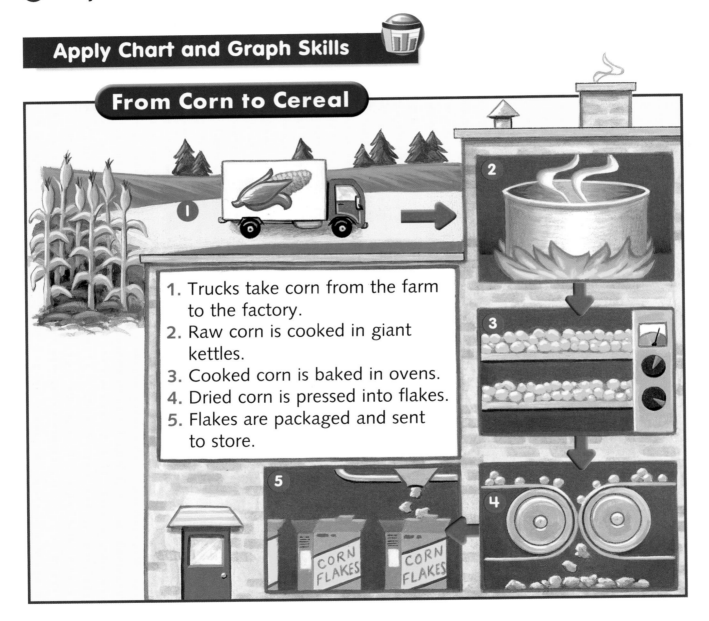

From Corn to Cereal

1. Trucks take corn from the farm to the factory.
2. Raw corn is cooked in giant kettles.
3. Cooked corn is baked in ovens.
4. Dried corn is pressed into flakes.
5. Flakes are packaged and sent to store.

14 How does corn get to the factory?

15 How is raw corn cooked?

16 What happens after the corn is baked?

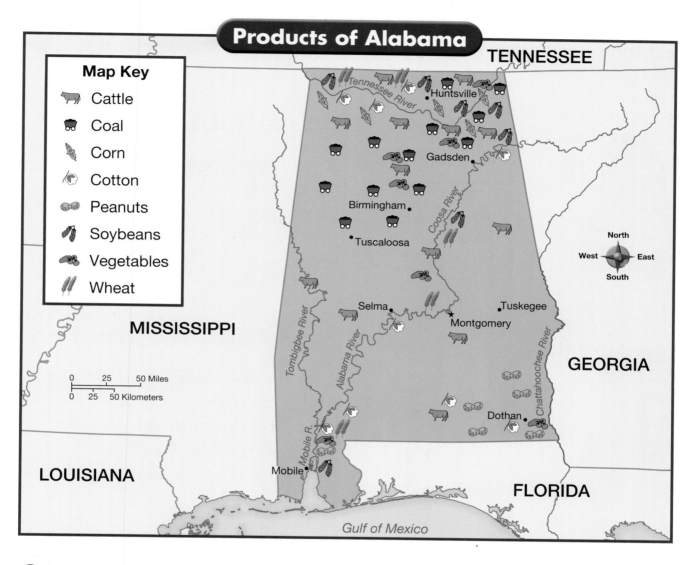

Products of Alabama

Map Key

- Cattle
- Coal
- Corn
- Cotton
- Peanuts
- Soybeans
- Vegetables
- Wheat

TENNESSEE

Tennessee River
Huntsville
Gadsden
Birmingham
Tuscaloosa
Coosa River

MISSISSIPPI

Tombigbee River
Alabama River
Selma
Montgomery
Tuskegee

North
West — East
South

GEORGIA

Chattahoochee River

0   25   50 Miles
0   25   50 Kilometers

LOUISIANA

Mobile R.
Mobile
Dothan

FLORIDA

Gulf of Mexico

17 What is the largest crop in Alabama?

18 In what part of Alabama is wheat grown?

19 Near what cities is coal found?

20 What crop is grown near Mobile?

Unit Activities

Complete the Unit Project Work in a group to plan a Career Day. Find out about the skills and tools people need to do their jobs.

GO ONLINE

Visit The Learning Site at **www.harcourtschool.com** for additional activities.

Choose Jobs

Gather information about different kinds of jobs.
- office jobs
- factory jobs
- service jobs
- sales jobs
- travel jobs
- outdoor jobs

Display Job Information

Set up booths to display information.
- Make pamphlets.
- Write job descriptions.
- Show pictures of workers.
- Invite guest speakers.

Visit Your Library

The Paperboy by Dav Pilkey. A boy enjoys the early morning as he delivers newspapers.

From Metal to Music by Wendy Davis. Follow the steps for making brass instruments.

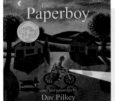

Market! by Ted Lewin. Read about marketplaces around the world and the goods they sell.

For Your Reference

Biographical Dictionary

The Biographical Dictionary lists many of the important people introduced in this book. The page number tells where the main discussion of each person starts. See the Index for other page references.

Anthony, Susan B. (1820–1906) Women's rights leader. She helped get women the same rights that men have. p. 83

Armstrong, Neil (1930–) American astronaut. He was the first person to walk on the moon. p. 220

Austen, Alice (1866–1952) Photographer. She took real-life photographs of immigrants. p. 27

Barton, Clara (1821–1912) Founder of the American Red Cross. She was its first president. p. 84

Bush, George W. (1946–) 43rd President of the United States. His father was the 41st President. p. 225

Carson, Rachel (1907–1964) American biologist and science writer. She told people about the dangers of pesticides. p. 249

Carter, Jimmy (1924–) and **Rosalynn** (1927–) Jimmy was the 39th President of the United States. He and his wife Rosalynn work for peace and justice. p. 297

Carver, George W. (1864–1943) African American scientist. He worked on ways to improve farming in the South. p. 133

Chavez, Cesar (1927–1993) American farm worker. He worked to get fair treatment for all farm workers. p. 85

Chavez, Dennis (1888–1962) Second Hispanic American to serve in the United States Senate. p. 249

Curie, Marie (1867–1934) French scientist. She was the first woman to win a Nobel Prize. p. 248

Earhart, Amelia (1897–1937?) American pilot. She was the first woman to fly across the Atlantic Ocean alone. p. 303

Einstein, Albert (1879–1955) One of the greatest scientists of all time. He wrote about time, space, and energy. p. 248

Fulton, Robert (1765–1815) American inventor and engineer. He is known for building a steamboat. p. 302

Gates, William (Bill) H. (1955–) Businessperson. He gives money to build and improve libraries and schools. p. 288

Glenn, John (1921–) First American astronaut to orbit Earth. p. 220

Grasso, Ella (1919–1981) First woman elected governor in the United States. p. 64

Greer, Pedro José (1956–) Florida doctor who started a walk-in clinic for people who are homeless. p. 86

Jefferson, Thomas (1743–1826) Third U.S. President. He wrote most of the Declaration of Independence. p. 244

Keller, Helen (1880–1968) American who overcame physical disabilities at an early age. She became a writer. p. 84

Key, Francis Scott (1779–1843) Lawyer and poet who wrote the words of "The Star-Spangled Banner." p. 77

Khan, Kublai (1216–1294) Ruler of China from 1279 to 1294. p. 59

King, Martin Luther, Jr. (1929–1968) African American civil rights leader. He received a Nobel Prize for working to change unfair laws. p. 248

Lincoln, Abraham (1809–1865) 16th President of the United States during the Civil War. He made it against the law to own slaves. p. 241

Ma, Yo-Yo (1955–) One of the world's most popular cello players. p. 87

Marshall, Thurgood (1908–1993) First African American justice of the United States Supreme Court. p. 246

Meir, Golda (1898–1978) Prime Minister of Israel from 1969 to 1974. p. 247

Mother Teresa (1910–1997) Roman Catholic nun who spent most of her life helping poor people. She received a Nobel Peace Prize. p. 85

Muñoz Marín, Luis (1898–1980) First elected governor of Puerto Rico. p. 249

Oñate, Juan de (1550?–1626?) Spanish explorer. He founded New Mexico. p. 229

Pasteur, Louis (1822–1895) French scientist who discovered that germs spread diseases. His work saved many lives. p. 247

Polo, Marco (1254–1324) Explorer from Venice, Italy. He traveled to Asia. p. 59

Ponce de León, Juan María (1460?–1521) Spanish explorer who explored what is now Florida. p. 231

Ramses II Egyptian pharaoh, or king. He built many temples. p. 58

Revere, Paul (1735–1818) Messenger who warned American leaders they were in danger from the British. p. 83

Rice, Condoleezza (1954–) Advisor to President George W. Bush. p. 86

Ride, Sally (1951–) Astronaut and first American woman in space. p. 175

Robinson, Jackie (1919–1972) First African American to play modern major league baseball. p. 82

Roosevelt, Eleanor (1884–1962) Wife of President Franklin Roosevelt. She worked for people in need around the world. p. 245

Roosevelt, Franklin (1882–1945) 32nd President of the United States. He was President longer than any other person. p. 64

Roosevelt, Theodore (1858–1919) 26th President of the United States. He protected natural resources and wilderness. p. 251

Sacagawea (1786?–1812?) Shoshone woman. She helped explorers Lewis and Clark communicate with Native Americans. p. 249

Shakespeare, William (1564–1616) English writer whose plays are still performed today. p. 12

Sitting Bull (1834?–1890) Sioux Indian leader. p. 249

Truth, Sojourner (1797?–1883) African American woman who spoke out against slavery. She was once a slave. p. 83

Washington, George (1732–1799) First President of the United States. He chose the place for the nation's capital city, Washington, D.C. p. 72

Picture Glossary

A

ancestor
A family member who lived a long time ago. My **ancestors** arrived here before my grandfather was born. (page 182)

anthem
The official song for a country. Our national **anthem** is played at special events. (page 76)

ancient
Very old. The pyramids are **ancient** buildings in Egypt. (page 216)

appoint
To name or choose for a public office or job. The President **appoints** helpers. (page 61)

artifact

An object from another time or place. This **artifact** was found in Greece. (page 224)

bar graph

A graph that uses bars to show how many or how much. This **bar graph** shows the money I saved each month. (page 184)

ballot

A piece of paper that shows the choices for voting. The voter marked her choices on the **ballot**. (page 62)

barter

To trade goods and services. People can **barter** instead of using money. (page 292)

bank

A business that looks after people's money. People put money in the **bank** to keep it safe. (page 287)

blizzard

A heavy snowstorm. The **blizzard** covered the roads with snow. (page 144)

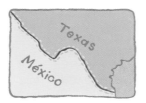

border

A line on a map that shows where a state or country ends. The red line shows the **border** between Texas and Mexico. (page 68)

capital

A city in which a state's or country's government meets and works. Washington, D.C., is the **capital** of the United States. (page 68)

business

The making or selling of goods or services. My parents have their own **business** selling flowers. (page 276)

cardinal directions

The main directions of north, south, east, and west. The **cardinal directions** help you find places on a map. (page 124)

calendar

A chart that shows the days, weeks, and months in a year. The **calendar** shows there are seven days in a week. (page 30)

cause

What makes something happen. My cat's action was the **cause** of a spill. (page 234)

318

change
To become different. The leaves **change** color when the weather gets cooler. (page 26)

climate
The kind of weather a place has over a long time. The rain forest has a very wet **climate**. (page 143)

citizen
A person who lives in and belongs to a community. Nick is a **citizen** of the United States. (page 8)

colony
A place that is ruled by another country. Virginia was the first English **colony** in America. (page 238)

city
A very large town. There are many tall buildings in my **city**. (page 20)

communication
The sharing of ideas and information. The firefighter uses a radio for **communication** with other firefighters. (page 196)

community
A group of people who live or work together in the same place. My family has lived in our **community** for many years. (page 6)

consequence
Something that happens because of what a person does. The **consequence** of wearing muddy shoes is a dirty floor. (page 49)

compass rose
Arrows on a map that show direction. The **compass rose** shows directions. (page 126)

conservation
Working to save resources or make them last longer. **Conservation** of electricity is a good idea. (page 148)

Congress
The group of citizens chosen to make decisions for the country. **Congress** votes on new laws. (page 71)

Constitution
The plan of government for the United States. The **Constitution** says every adult citizen has the right to vote. (page 73)

320

consumer

A person who buys and uses goods and services. This **consumer** is buying food for a picnic. (page 279)

council

A group of citizens chosen to make decisions for all the people. The **council** is discussing where to build the playground. (page 53)

continent

One of the seven main land areas on the Earth. We live on the **continent** of North America. (page 122)

country

An area of land with its own people and laws. We are proud of our **country**. (page 22)

cooperate

To work together. My family likes to **cooperate** on projects. (page 16)

court

A place where a judge decides whether a person has broken the law, and if so, what the consequence should be. Mr. Jackson broke the law and had to go to **court**. (page 54)

crop
A plant people grow for food or other needs. Corn is an important **crop** in the United States. (page 132)

 D

decision
A choice. Tom made a **decision** about what shirt to buy. (page 152)

culture
A group's way of life. Music and dance are part of my **culture**. (page 169)

desert
A large, dry area of land. Very little rain falls in the **desert**. (page 108)

custom
A group's way of doing something. One Hawaiian **custom** is to give flowers to visitors. (page 186)

My favorite hobby is finding rocks. I have 143 different rocks. I keep them in boxes.

detail
An extra piece of information about something. The number of rocks Sara has is a **detail**. (page 10)

diagram

A drawing that shows the parts of something or explains how it works. The **diagram** helped me put my toy together. (page 256)

equator

An imaginary line that divides Earth in half between north and south. Most of South America is south of the **equator**. (page 125)

effect

What happens because of a cause. My cat was surprised by the **effect** of its action. (page 234)

explorer

A person who goes first to find out about a place. Lewis and Clark were famous **explorers**. (page 172)

election

A time when people vote for their leaders. The **election** to choose the President is held in November. (page 60)

fact

A piece of information that is true. It is a **fact** that humans have walked on the moon. (page 88)

factory

A building in which people use machines to make goods. The car was made in a **factory** in Detroit. (page 282)

forest

A very large area of trees. This is a **forest** of pine trees. (page 140)

fair

Done in a way that is right and honest. To be **fair**, my brother pours and I choose the glass I want. (page 8)

freedom

The right of people to make their own choices. Americans have the **freedom** to vote. (page 238)

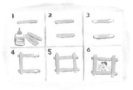

flow chart

A chart that shows the steps needed to make or do something. The **flow chart** shows how to make a picture frame. (page 284)

free enterprise

The freedom to start and run any kind of business. **Free enterprise** helps these children earn money. (page 286)

fuel

A resource, such as oil, that can be burned for heat or energy. Gasoline is a **fuel** used in cars. (page 141)

goods

Things that can be bought and sold. This store sells many kinds of **goods**. (page 272)

geography

The study of Earth and its people. **Geography** teaches us about Earth and the people on it. (page 100)

government

The group of citizens that runs a community, state, or country. Our **government** needs strong leaders. (page 47)

globe

A model of Earth. We can find countries on our classroom **globe**. (page 124)

government service

A service that a government provides for citizens. Police officers provide a **government service**. (page 55)

governor
The leader of a state's government. Every state has a **governor**. (page 64)

hero
A person who has done something brave or important. This **hero** saved someone's life. (page 244)

gulf
A large body of ocean water that is partly surrounded by land. The **Gulf** of Mexico is between Mexico and the United States. (page 118)

hill
Land that rises above the land around it. It is fun to slide down a snowy **hill** in winter. (page 112)

heritage
The culture and traditions handed down to people by their ancestors. My grandmother teaches me about my **heritage**. (page 178)

history
The study of what happened to people in the past. The **history** of our country is interesting. (page 222)

history map

A map that shows how a place looked in an earlier time. This **history map** shows the original thirteen colonies. (page 242)

income

The money people earn for the work they do. Miguel will use his **income** to buy lemonade. (page 286)

holiday

A day to celebrate or remember something. Many African Americans celebrate a **holiday** called Kwanzaa. (page 186)

independence

The freedom of people to choose their own government. George Washington fought for **independence**. (page 238)

immigrant

A person who comes from somewhere else to live in a country. My great-grandfather was an Irish **immigrant**. (page 174)

interest

Money that money earns in a bank. My savings have earned **interest**. (page 287)

island

A landform with water all around it. Deep blue water surrounds the **island**. (page 115)

lake

A body of water that has land all around it. We enjoy fishing in the **lake**. (page 117)

judge

The leader of a court. The **judge** punished the lawbreaker. (page 54)

landform

A kind of land with a special shape, such as a mountain, hill, or plain. A mountain is a large **landform**. (page 112)

justice

Fairness. Americans believe in **justice**. (page 85)

landmark

A familiar object at a place. The Alamo is a Texas **landmark**. (page 239)

language
The words or signs people use to communicate. Some people use sign **language** to communicate. (page 190)

location
The place where something is. The map will help you find your **location**. (page 19)

law
A rule that people in a community must follow. A speed limit **law** keeps people safe. (page 48)

main idea
What the information you are reading is mostly about. Every paragraph should have a **main idea**. (page 10)

legislature
A group of citizens chosen to make decisions for a state. The **legislature** will decide where to build a new road. (page 65)

maize
A kind of corn. **Maize** is one crop grown in Mexico. (page 255)

329

majority rule

Rule by more than half of the people in a community. Building a new school was decided by **majority rule**. (page 62)

map grid

A set of columns and rows placed on a map to help people find a location. The star is at square C-3 on the **map grid**. (page 250)

manufacture

To make with machines. Robots are used to **manufacture** car parts. (page 283)

map key

The part of a map that shows what the symbols mean. Look for the symbol of the bridge in the **map key**. (page 24)

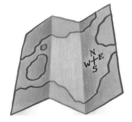

map

A drawing that shows where places are. Can you find an island on this **map**? (page 19)

map scale

The part of a map that helps you find distance. The **map scale** can help you find out how far it is from Charleston to Elkins. (page 146)

map symbol

A small picture that stands for a real thing on Earth. This **map symbol** stands for a mountain. (page 24)

modern

Of the present time. **Modern** technology helps us do our jobs. (page 216)

mayor

The leader of a city or town government. The **mayor** makes important decisions for our community. (page 52)

monument

A statue or marker created to honor a person or an event. This **monument** honors George Washington. (page 244)

memorial

A monument created to honor and remember a hero. This **memorial** reminds us of a brave American. (page 244)

mountain

The highest kind of land. The eagle soared over the top of the **mountain**. (page 114)

museum

A building in which objects from other times and places are displayed. Famous paintings hang in this **museum**. (page 228)

neighborhood

The part of a community in which a group of people lives. The people in my **neighborhood** are friendly. (page 18)

natural resource

Something found in nature that people can use to meet their needs. Oil is a **natural resource**. (page 128)

ocean

A very large body of salty water. Ships sail across the **ocean**. (page 109)

needs

Things people must have to live. Food, clothing, and a place to live are **needs**. (page 32)

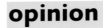

opinion

A statement of what a person believes to be true but cannot prove. My friend and I have different **opinions** about the movie. (page 88)

P

papyrus

A kind of paper made from a certain kind of plant. Ancient Egyptians wrote on **papyrus**. (page 252)

peace

A time of quietness and calm when people are getting along. We wish everyone could live in **peace**. (page 78)

patriotic symbol

A picture or object that stands for something the people of a country believe in. The bald eagle is a **patriotic symbol** for our country. (page 74)

peninsula

A landform that has water on only three sides. Part of Florida is a **peninsula**. (page 115)

patriotism

A feeling of pride people have for their country. People show **patriotism** when they wave the flag. (page 74)

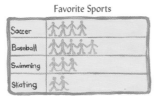

picture graph

A graph that uses pictures to stand for numbers of things. The **picture graph** shows that baseball got the most votes as favorite sport. (page 80)

pioneer

A person who is one of the first to live in a new land. Many **pioneers** traveled west in covered wagons. (page 173)

pollution

Anything that makes the air, land, or water dirty. Throwing garbage into a river causes **pollution**. (page 150)

plain

Land that is mostly flat. Fields of crops stretch across the **plain**. (page 113)

predict

To say what will happen. Forecasters **predict** snow today. [Sandy's team won!] (page 226)

point of view

A way of thinking about something. I have a different **point of view** from my sister. (page 170)

President

Leader of the United States government. George W. Bush is **President** of the United States. (page 72)

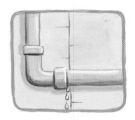

problem

Something difficult or hard to understand. The **problem** with the pipe is that it leaks. (page 50)

product map

A map that shows where products are found or made. This **product map** shows where corn is grown. (page 304)

producer

A person who makes, grows, or sells goods. This **producer** grows fruit to sell. (page 277)

property

Something that belongs to a person or group. This park is public **property**. (page 67)

product

Something that is made by nature or by people. Applesauce is a **product** made from apples. (page 284)

public service

Work done for the good of the community. Police officers give a **public service** by protecting citizens. (page 86)

PICTURE GLOSSARY

raw material

A resource used to make a product. Wood is a **raw material** used to make furniture. (page 281)

region

An area. We live in a mountain **region**. (page 242)

recreation

The things people do in their spare time, such as playing sports or having hobbies. Sailing is my favorite kind of **recreation**. (page 164)

religion

A belief in a god or gods. Americans enjoy freedom of **religion**. (page 180)

recycle

To use things again. We can **recycle** newspapers to make new paper. (page 149)

responsibility

Something that a citizen should take care of or do. It is my **responsibility** to take these glasses I found to the store owner. (page 9)

rights

Freedoms. Freedom of speech is one of our many **rights**. (page 73)

route

A way to go from one place to another. The **route** on this map is easy to follow. (page 176)

river

A stream of water that flows across the land. The Mississippi **River** is the longest river in the United States. (page 116)

rule

An instruction telling what must or must not be done. There is a **rule** against talking loudly in the library. (page 8)

role

The part a person plays in a group or community. The **role** of a goalie is to keep the other team from scoring. (page 12)

S

scarce

Not in good supply, or hard to find. When money is **scarce**, George cannot buy candy. (page 290)

scribe

A person who records things in writing. Long ago, a **scribe** wrote in clay. (page 252)

settlement

A small community started in a new place. The pioneers built a **settlement**. (page 242)

season

One of the four parts of the year that have different kinds of weather. My favorite **season** is fall. (page 212)

settler

One of the first people to make a home in a new place. The **settler** worked hard on his land. (page 230)

services

Work done for others for money. We paid the waiter for his **services**. (page 274)

solution

The way people agree to solve a problem. The **solution** to the leaky pipe is to replace it. (page 50)

source

The place where something comes from. An encyclopedia is a good **source** of information. (page 222)

Supreme Court

The highest court in the United States. The **Supreme Court** decides the most important cases. (page 73)

state

A part of a country. Texas is one of our fifty **states**. (page 22)

table

A chart that shows information in rows and columns. A **table** can be used to compare things. (page 134)

suburb

A community near a large city. This **suburb** is about thirty miles from the city. (page 21)

tax

Money paid to the government that is used to pay for services. The **tax** we pay at the store helps pay for building roads. (page 56)

technology

The use of new inventions in everyday life. Computers are a useful **technology**. (page 136)

trade

The exchange of one thing for another. Is this a fair **trade**? (page 298)

time line

A line that shows when events happen. This **time line** shows holidays. (page 220)

tradition

A way of doing something that is passed on from parents to children. Wearing kilts is a Scottish **tradition**. (page 181)

tornado

A strong, whirling wind that causes great damage to land and buildings. A **tornado** is a dangerous storm. (page 144)

transportation

Ways of carrying people and goods from one place to another. Buses and airplanes are two types of **transportation**. (page 300)

unique
One-of-a-kind. Would you say this painting is **unique**? (page 168)

vote
A choice that gets counted. The person who gets the most **votes** is the winner. (page 60)

valley
Low land between hills or mountains, often with a river or stream flowing through it. A small river runs through the **valley**. (page 114)

wants
Things people would like to have but do not need. I have more **wants** than I can afford. (page 33)

volunteer
A person who works without being paid. I am a **volunteer** for my favorite charity. (page 296)

Index

INDEX

INDEX

INDEX

For permission to reprint copyrighted material, grateful acknowledgment is made to the following sources:

Charlesbridge Publishing, Inc.: Cover illustration from *Different Just Like Me* by Lori Mitchell. Copyright © 1999 by Lori Mitchell.

Cobblehill Books, an affiliate of Dutton Children's Books, a division of Penguin Putnam Inc.: Cover photograph from *Chidi Only Likes Blue: An African Book of Colors* by Ifeoma Onyefulu. Photograph copyright © 1997 by Ifeoma Onyefulu.

Farrar, Straus and Giroux, LLC: Cover illustration by Tom Pohrt from *The Tomb of the Boy King* by John Frank. Illustration copyright © 2001 by Tom Pohrt.

Harcourt, Inc.: Cover illustration by Thomas Locker from *Between Earth and Sky: Legends of Native American Sacred Places* by Joseph Bruchac. Illustration copyright © 1996 by Thomas Locker. Cover illustration from *Moon Rope* by Lois Ehlert. Copyright © 1992 by Lois Ehlert. From *Worksong* by Gary Paulsen, illustrated by Ruth Wright Paulsen. Text copyright © 1997 by Gary Paulsen; illustrations copyright © 1997 by Ruth Wright Paulsen.

HarperCollins Publishers: From *The Egyptian Cinderella* by Shirley Climo, illustrated by Ruth Heller. Text copyright © 1989 by Shirley Climo; illustrations copyright © 1989 by Ruth Heller. From *The Korean Cinderella* by Shirley Climo, illustrated by Ruth Heller. Text copyright © 1993 by Shirley Climo; illustrations copyright © 1993 by Ruth Heller. Cover illustration by Bethanne Andersen from *Kindle Me a Riddle: A Pioneer Story* by Roberta Karim. Illustration copyright © 1999 by Bethanne Andersen. Cover illustration from *Market!* by Ted Lewin. Copyright © 1996 by Ted Lewin. Cover photograph by Comstock Inc./David Lokey from *Teamwork* by Ann Morris. Photograph © by Comstock Inc./David Lokey. Cover illustration by Lynn Sweat from *Amelia Bedelia 4 Mayor* by Herman Parish. Illustration copyright © 1999 by Lynn Sweat. From *Some Things Go Together* by Charlotte Zolotow, cover illustration by Karen Gundersheimer. Text copyright © 1969 by Charlotte Zolotow; illustration copyright © 1983 by Karen Gundersheimer.

Holiday House, Inc.: Cover illustration from *Celebrate the 50 States!* by Loreen Leedy. Copyright © 1999 by Loreen Leedy.

Henry Holt and Company, Inc.: Cover illustration from *Chinatown* by William Low. Copyright © 1997 by William Low.

Houghton Mifflin Company: Cover illustration by John Clapp from *Right Here on This Spot* by Sharon Hart Addy. Illustration copyright © 1999 by John Clapp.

Alfred A. Knopf Children's Books, a division of Random House, Inc.: Cover illustration by Reynold Ruffins from *Misoso: Once Upon a Time Tales from Africa* by Verna Aardema. Illustration copyright © 1994 by Reynold Ruffins. Cover illustration by Michael McCurdy from *American Tall Tales* by Mary Pope Osborne. Illustration copyright © 1991 by Michael McCurdy.

Little, Brown and Company (Inc.): Cover illustration from *Bravo, Maurice!* by Rebecca Bond. Copyright © 2000 by Rebecca Bond. Cover illustration by Kathy Jakobsen from *This Land Is Your Land* by Woody Guthrie. Illustration copyright © 1998 by Kathy Jakobsen. Cover illustration by Isabelle Brent from *The Golden Bird*, retold from the Brothers Grimm by Neil Philip. Illustration copyright © 1995 by Isabelle Brent.

The Millbrook Press, Inc., Brookfield, CT 06804: Cover illustration by Elisa Kleven from *Our Big Home: An Earth Poem* by Linda Glaser. Illustration copyright © 2000 by Elisa Kleven.

Joan Miller: From "Valentine For Earth" in *The Little Naturalist* by Frances Frost. Text copyright © 1959 by the Estate of Frances Frost; © renewed 1987.

G. P. Putnam's Sons, an imprint of Penguin Putnam Books for Young Readers, a division of Penguin Putnam Inc.: Cover illustration from *Officer Buckle and Gloria* by Peggy Rathmann. Copyright © 1995 by Peggy Rathmann. From *Growing Seasons* by Elsie Lee Splear, cover illustration by Ken Stark. Text and cover copyright © 2000 by Carolyn Spear Pratt.

Scholastic Inc.: Cover illustration from *The Paperboy* by Dav Pilkey. Copyright © 1996 by Dav Pilkey. Published by Orchard Books, an imprint of Scholastic Inc. *Tulip Sees America* by Cynthia Rylant, illustrated by Lisa Desimini. Text copyright © 1998 by Cynthia Rylant; illustrations copyright © 1998 by Lisa Desimini. Published by The Blue Sky Press, an imprint of Scholastic Inc.

Sports Illustrated For Kids: From "Eskimo Games" by Andrew Gutelle, illustrated by Brad Hamann in *Sports Illustrated For Kids*, April 1993. Copyright © 1993 by Time Inc.

Viking Penguin, an imprint of Penguin Putnam Books for Young Readers, a division of Penguin Putnam Inc.: Cover illustration by S. D. Schindler from *Are We There Yet, Daddy?* by Virginia Walters. Illustration copyright © 1999 by S. D. Schindler.

Albert Whitman & Company: Cover illustration by Cornelius Van Wright and Ying-Hwa Hu from *Mei-Mei Loves the Morning* by Margaret Holloway Tsubakiyama. Illustration copyright © 1999 by Cornelius Van Wright and Ying-Hwa Hu.

ILLUSTRATION CREDITS:

ATLAS

Page A1-A13, MAPQUEST.COM.; A12, Studio Liddell.

UNIT 1

Page 4-5, Brenda Joysmith; 8-9, Laura Ovresat; 11, Renee Preston; 14, Jennifer Dingess; 19, Ken Batelman/Brian Ashe; 22-23, Ken Batelman; 24-25, 39 Stephanie Darden.

UNIT 2

Pages 44-45, Andy Cook; 50-51, Darin Johnston; 63, Renee Preston; 81 Stephanie Darden.

UNIT 3

Page 100-112, Lisa Desimini; 130, Jon Edwards; 135, Ken Batelman/Brian Ashe; 160, Wendy Walenberg.

UNIT 4

Page 206, Stephanie Darden; 208, Renee Preston.

UNIT 5

Pages 212-215, Doug Bowles; 218, 256-257, 262, Jon Edwards; 237, Wayne Still; 251, Stephanie Darden.

UNIT 6

Page 268-271, Ruth Wright Paulsen; 299, Ken Batelman/Stephanie Darden; 300-301, Studio Liddell; 310, Scott Schiedly.

PICTURE GLOSSARY

Page 316, 317, 318, 319, 320, 321, Denise Fraifeld; 316, 322, 325, 331, 332, 333, 334, 335, 336, 337, 338, Franklin Ayers; 317, 326, 327, 336, 337, 338, Everett Magie; 318, 322, 323, 324, 325, 327, 328, 329, Robert Dellinger; 318, 319, 320, 329, 330, 333, Steven Royal; 321, 326, 327, 336, 337, 338, 339, 340, 341, Navin Patel; 330, 333, 340, Darrin Johnston.

PHOTO CREDITS

Cover: Doug DuKane (fireman, fire engine); Rafael Macia/Photo Researchers, Inc. (flag); Ed Castle/Folio (building).

PAGE PLACEMENT KEY: (t)-top (c) center, (b)-bottom, (l)-left, (r)-right, (bg) background, (fg)-foreground;

TITLE PAGE AND TABLE OF CONTENTS: iv Shelburne Museum; v Terry Heffernan Films; vi The Chester County Historical Society, vii Superstock; viii Smithsonian Institution;

UNIT 1

Opener (fg) Shelburne Museum, 1 Shelburne Museum; 2 (tr) Joseph Sohm, Chromosohm/Corbis; 2 (br) Ted Rose/Unicorn Stock Photos; 3 (cr) Bob Daemmrich/The Image Works; 6,7 (b) Panoramic Images; 6 J. Sohm/The Image Works; 7 (tl)(tr) PhotoVault.com; 7 (cr) Jay Taffet/Affordable Aerials.com; 8 (tr) Cathy Fox Raphaelson/Houserstock; 8 (bl) M.Anyman/The Image Works, Inc.; 8 (br) Bob Daemmrich Photos; 8 (cl) John P. Kelley/The Image Bank; 8 Steve Jessmore/Dembinsky Photo Associates; 8 (cr) Peter Essick/Aurora /PictureQuest; 9 (tr) A. Ramey/Stock, Boston; 9 (cr) M. Ferguson/PhotoEdit; 9 (cr) Frozen Images/The Image Works, Inc.; 18 (b), (c) Richard Hamilton Smith Photography; 20 (cr) C. E. Mitchell/Black Star; 21 (b) Jeff Greenberg/Unicorn Stock Photos; 26 (br) Eric & Nathalie Cumbie; 26 (cr) Eric & Nathalie Cumbie, 27 © Eric & Nathalie Cumbie; 27 (tr) Staten Island Historical Society; 27 Siede Preis/PhotoDisc; 28 (l) The Mariners Museum/Corbis; (r) E.O Hoppe/Corbis; 29 Stephen Morton/Getty Images; 30 (tl), (cl) Culver Pictures/Picture Quest; 32 (c) Ecoscene/Corbis; 32 and 33 (b) Kelvin Murray/Stone; 32 (cl), (bl) David & Peter Turnley/Corbis; 32 (cl), (bl) Jason Laure/Laure Communications; 33 (c) Aaron Haupt/Photo Researchers; 33 (tl) Spencer Grant/PhotoEdit 33 (tr) Loren Santow/Stone; 33 (cr) Yann Guichaoua/Allsport Photography; 34-35 (c) PhotoEdit; 34 (br) Judith F. Baca/Great Wall Images; 35 (tl) Sparc Murals; 35 (tr) PhotoEdit.

UNIT 2

Opener (fg) Terry Heffernan Films, (bg) Wilton S. Tifft Photography, (spread) Wilton S. Tifft Photography; 41 Terry Heffernan Films; 42 (tl) Mark Morgan/Black Star/Harcourt; 42 (tl) Bob Daemmrich/The Image Works; 43 (tl) Mark Burnett/Stock, Boston; 43 (cr) Bob Daemmrich/The Image Works; 48-49 Spencer Grant/PhotoEdit; 52 (c) Kelly Culpepper/Harcourt; 52 Ron Wurzer/Getty Images; 53 (t) Ron Wurzer/Getty Images; 53 (br) Mark Richards/PhotoEdit; 53 (cr) Candace C. Mundy/Tampa Tribune/Silver Image; 54 Bob Daemmrich/Stock, Boston; 55 (t) Michael Leschisin/Silver Image; 55 (b) David R. Frazier; 56 (t) Image Farm/PictureQuest; 56 Eric Berndt/Unicorn Stock Photos; 57 (t) Steven

Resource; 252 (br) Newberry Library, Chicago/Superstock; 253 (t) David Forbert/Superstock; 253 (c) Peter Harholdt/Superstock; 253 (b) Superstock; 254 (t) Macduff Everton/The Image Works, Inc.; 254 (b) Newberry Library, Chicago; 255 Michael J. Pettypool/Houserstock, Inc.; 256 Karen Roush; 257 (br) Hulton/Archive Photos; 258 (bl) Museum of the City of New York/Corbis; 258 (bcl) The Granger Collection, New York; 258 (bcr) The Granger Collection, New York; 258 (br) The Granger Collection, New York; 258-259 Paul A. Souders/Corbis; 259 (tr) Lionel Green/Archive Photos.

UNIT 6

Opener (bg) Aneal N. Vohra/Unicorn Stock Photos, (spread) Aneal N. Vohra/Unicorn Stock Photos; 266 (tl) David Butow/Corbis SABA; 267 (tl) Superstock; 267 (cr) Randy Vaughn-Dotta/AGStock USA; 272 (tc) Michael Newman/PhotoEdit; 272 (tr) PhotoEdit; 272 (cl) Joel W. Rogers/Corbis; 272 (c) Bob Daemmrich

Photos; 272 (bc) Pictor; 272 (br) Bob Daemmrich Photos; 273 (tl) Matthew Borkoski/Stock, Boston; 273 (bl) Bob Daemmrich Photos; 273 (r) Daniel Grogan/Pictor; 274 (tl) Bob Daemmrich Photos; 274 (c) Superstock; 274 (bl) Karen Roush; 274 (br) PhotoEdit; 275 (tr) Bill Gallery/Stock, Boston; 275 (c) VCG/FPG International; 275 (bl) Bob Daemmrich/The Image Works; 275 (bg) David Wagner/Phototake/PictureQuest; 280 (both) McGuire Studio Midwest; 280-281 John Colwell/Grant Heilman Photography; 281 (t) John Colwell/Grant Heilman Photography; 281 (c) McGuire Studio Midwest; 282, 283, 284, 285, McGuire Studio Midwest; 288 (b) Reuters NewMedia Inc./Corbis; 289 (tr) Karen Roush; 292 (cr) Museum of the City of New York Toy Collection; 292 (bl), (br) British Museum; 293 (tl) W.S. Nawrocki/Nawrocki Stock Photo; 293 (tl) British Museum; 293 (c) Larry Stevens/Nawrocki Stock Photo; 293 (bl), (br) British Museum; 294 (tl), (tr) Feldman & Associates; 294 (c), (cl) Smithsonian Institution National Numismatic Collection; 294 (cr) Feldman & Associates; 294

(bl) AFP/Corbis; 294 (bl) Corbis; 294 (br) Smithsonian Institution National Numismatic Collection; 296 (cr) Richard T. Nowitz/Corbis; 296 (bl) Bob Daemmrich Photos; 297 Mark Peterson/Corbis SABA; 300 Pictor; 301 (tl) Bob Daemmrich Photos; 301 (tr) Joseph Sohm;ChromoSohm Inc./Corbis; 302 (tr) Ian Clark/International Stock; 302 (c) Bob Daemmrich Photos; 302 (b) (inset) The Granger Collection, New York; 302 (br) Paul A. Souders/Corbis; 303 (tr) Corbis; 306 (l) Gale Zucker; 303 (r) Joe Towers/Corbis Stock Market; 306 (cr) Gale Zucker 2001; 307 (tr) Gale Zucker 2001; 307 (c) Binney & Smith Inc.; 307 (b) Gale Zucker 2001.

All other photos by Harcourt Photographers, Ken Kinzie, Weronica Ankarorn, Victoria Bowen, and US Color.